Unlocking Your Fortune

A 12-Month Guide tc Achieving Six-Figure Success

Linda K. Caldwell

“Unlocking Your Fortune”

Dedication

To my beloved husband, whose unwavering support and love inspire me each day.

To my mother, whose strength and wisdom have shaped me into who I am.

To my cherished father and my two dear brothers, whose memories will forever guide my journey.

To my wonderful daughters, may you always chase your dreams with courage and heart.

And to my amazing sisters and the rest of my family, thank you for your love and support.

This book is for all of you~~who fill my life with purpose and joy.

Acknowledgements

I would like to express my heartfelt gratitude to my husband, Wesley Caldwell, whose unwavering support and encouragement have been my guiding light.

To my wonderful children, Stephanie, Courtenay, Urell, Jade, and Noah, your love and laughter inspire me every day.

To my precious grandchildren, thank you for bringing joy to my life.

To my loving mother, Linda Cooper, your strength and wisdom have always been a source of inspiration.

To my sisters, Monica and Renea, your love and support uplift me every day.

Additionally, to my entire family, extended family, and friends, your encouragement has meant the world to me.

I am also deeply grateful to my dear friend and attorney, Dr. Kim Beaton, for her invaluable guidance and support.

A special thanks to Logo Web Solutions/UBP and the team for your invaluable assistance in bringing this book to life. Lastly, to my readers, I hope this book resonates with you as much as it did with me.

Thank you all.

Contents

1

Discovering Your True Potential

Explore Your Path to Prosperity

Before you dive into business plans, branding, or any clever strategy, you have to start with the one thing that drives it all: you.

Let's be honest—most of us are in such a rush to "make it" that we skip over the one step that matters most: figuring out who we are and what we actually want. We follow trends, sign up for courses, mimic what's worked for other people—but never stop to ask if the path we're on fits us at all.

This first chapter is here to help you pause and get clear. Not vague "follow your dreams" clear, but real, grounded clarity. What are you good at? What drives you? What kind of life are you really trying to build—not just in theory, but day-to-day?

You might be surprised at what you find. Sometimes we've buried our strengths under years of expectations or fear. Sometimes we've never even thought about what success looks like beyond "more money" or "freedom." But if you don't know what you're aiming for, how do you know when you've arrived?

We'll start by looking inward—at your strengths, your passions, and the kind of life you're wired to thrive in. Then we'll look at where you are now and what's standing in the way. You'll get a chance to challenge some of the stories you've picked up along the way, the ones that quietly limit how much you allow yourself to want—or receive.

Finally, we'll talk about the version of you who can build and live out that six-figure success, and what it looks like to step into that identity now—not someday.

This chapter isn't about hype. It's about alignment. When you know who you are and what you're working toward, everything else becomes clearer and easier to navigate. Let's start there.

Identify Your Core Strengths, Passions, and Purpose

Here's the thing: Most people can tell you what they're not good at faster than what they are good at. We're trained from a young age to fix flaws instead of nurture gifts. But if you want to build a business—or a life—that leads to real success, you need to know your strengths like a chef knows their ingredients.

So, ask yourself:

- What comes naturally to me?
- When do I feel most alive, most "in flow"?
- What kind of problems do people always come to me to solve?

Your strengths aren't just talents—they're clues. They point to the path of least resistance. And when you align those strengths with your passions (what you love doing) and your purpose (why you're doing it), you unlock the most potent form of momentum: meaningful motivation.

If you're passionate about helping others, and your strength is communication, your path might involve coaching, teaching, or storytelling. If you're analytical and love solving puzzles, maybe you're meant to build systems, optimize businesses, or turn data into gold.

This is not about chasing trends or copying someone else's formula. This is about rooting your pursuit of wealth in who you truly are. Because the most successful people aren't just talented—they're aligned. They know what they bring to the table, and they sit at the right table because of it.

Try This:

Make Three Lists:

1. Things I'm naturally good at
2. Things I love doing (even if I don't get paid for it yet)
3. Times I've felt truly proud or fulfilled

Now look for the overlap. That's your power zone.

Your six-figure journey won't be built by being someone else. It starts with owning who you already are—fully.

Conduct a Personal Success Audit: Where You Are vs. Where You Want to Be

Let's pause and look at where things actually stand—not where you wish they were, not where you told people they were, but where they really are. No guilt, no drama. Just an honest check-in.

Start with the basics: How's your income? Your energy levels? Your time? Are you building something that excites you, or are you stuck in survival mode? Do your daily actions reflect the future you say you want? Or are you going through the motions and hoping things will eventually click?

This isn't about beating yourself up. It's about getting honest enough to make decisions that actually move you forward. You can't make progress if you're fuzzy on the facts. Think of this like a GPS—if you don't know your starting point, it doesn't matter how fancy the destination is. You'll just stay stuck.

Now flip it. Where do you want to be? And not just financially—what do you want your life to look and feel like? Be specific. How do you spend your mornings? What kind of work are you doing? How much are you earning? Who are you working with—or for?

Clarity gives direction. And direction helps you make better decisions. When you know where you are and where you're going, you can see the gap between them. And that gap? That's the work. That's your map.

So take the time to do this. Write it down. Be real about what's working and what's not. The goal isn't to feel bad about where you are—it's to take ownership so you can start changing it.

Clarify Your Vision of Financial Freedom and What Six-Figure Success Looks Like to You

Let's talk about what you actually want—not what social media says you should want, not what sounds impressive in a group chat, but what you really need for life to feel right.

The number "six figures" gets thrown around a lot, but it doesn't mean the same thing for everyone. For some, it means quitting a job and working for themselves. For others, it's about having options—less stress, more flexibility, or enough saved to breathe a little easier.

So—what does financial freedom look like in your life?

Try to move past the dollar signs and dig into what those dollars are meant to unlock. Do you want to travel more? Be home in time for dinner? Pay off debt? Build something that matters to you? Maybe you just want to stop living paycheck to paycheck and finally have room to plan ahead.

Don't overthink it—just be honest. If you could build a version of life that feels secure, free, and meaningful, what would be in it? What would be out of it?

Grab a notebook and write it down in simple language. Forget buzzwords like "financial independence" or "generational wealth" for now. Just paint a clear picture of a life that works for you.

This step matters more than people realize. When you define what success means on your terms, it becomes easier to stay focused. You'll spend less time chasing someone else's goals and more time building something that actually fits. That kind of clarity is worth more than any strategy.

Overcome Limiting Beliefs That Block Abundance

Sometimes the biggest thing standing between you and success isn't a lack of skill or opportunity—it's the voice in your head telling you you're not ready, not capable, or not the kind of person who gets to have more.

These thoughts don't always sound dramatic. They slip in quietly, like:

> "People like me don't make that kind of money."
> "If I earn more, I'll lose everything else that matters."
> "I'm not smart or confident enough to run my own business."

These are called limiting beliefs. And while they're often based on old stories—things you heard growing up or learned from hard experiences—they're not facts. They're just thoughts you've repeated often enough to believe.

Start by paying attention to what you tell yourself when you hit resistance. Are you assuming things won't work out for you? That you'll mess it up? That people won't take you seriously?

Write those beliefs down. See them for what they are—patterns, not truths. Then challenge them.

Ask: Is this actually true? Do I have proof? What would I believe instead if I were starting fresh today?

You don't have to force yourself to feel positive all the time. Just start questioning the stories that keep you stuck. Every time you catch a limiting belief and replace it with something more honest or useful, you loosen its grip.

This is ongoing work. But the more you do it, the easier it becomes to take action without second-guessing yourself every step of the way. Success isn't just about learning new things—it's about unlearning the lies you've been carrying.

Create a Success Identity: Who Must You Become to Earn Six Figures?

Here's the truth—not much changes in your life until you do.

You can have the right strategy, the perfect plan, and all the tools. But if you still think, speak, and act like the person who's stuck or unsure, you'll keep getting the same results. Six-figure success doesn't just show up because you want it. It shows up when your choices, habits, and mindset start matching the person who's already living it.

So, who is that version of you?

What do they do differently each day? How do they talk about their work? How do they handle distractions, setbacks, or tough decisions? What do they stop tolerating?

This isn't about pretending or faking confidence. It's about stepping into the next version of yourself—on purpose. You're not inventing someone new. You're becoming more of who you were always capable of being.

Try this: Write a short description of the six-figure version of you. Include how they think, what they focus on, and what kind of choices they make. Then ask yourself, What would that version of me do next? And do it—even in small ways.

Change doesn't happen overnight, but it starts with acting like the person who's already arrived. One decision at a time, you build new patterns. Over time, those patterns shift your results. Not by chance, but by choice.

You don't earn six figures just by working harder. You earn it by becoming the kind of person who expects more—and follows through.

2

Crafting Your Business Blueprint

Designing the Roadmap to Success

A business doesn't succeed by chance. It succeeds because it's built on a clear, intentional plan—a blueprint that guides every decision. Without one, you end up reacting to problems instead of building something sustainable. This chapter is about laying that foundation.

Think of your blueprint as the roadmap for your next 12 months. It answers key questions: What will you sell? Who will you serve? Why will they choose you over someone else? And most importantly, how will you hit your financial targets without burning out or spinning in circles?

We'll start by looking at the type of business you want to run, because everything flows from there. Once you know whether you're selling products, services, or a mix of both, you can get specific about your audience, refine what makes you stand out, and set measurable goals. The final step is turning those ideas into a simple, actionable plan—one you can actually follow and adjust as you grow.

Clarity doesn't just save you time; it gives you confidence. When you know where you're going, you can stop second-guessing every move and start taking focused action. Let's begin by answering the first question every entrepreneur needs to face: *What's your business model?*

Choose Your Business Model: Product, Service, or Hybrid

Your business model is the foundation of your revenue. It defines *how* you'll make money and the kind of work you'll be doing day to day.

A product-based business sells physical or digital products—anything from clothing to e-books or online courses. Once created, products can be sold repeatedly, which makes them easier to scale, but they often require upfront time and investment.

- A **service-based business** sells expertise, time, or skills. Examples include consulting, coaching, or freelance work. Services are faster to start and usually have lower costs but can be harder to scale without systems.

- A **hybrid model** combines both—for instance, offering coaching plus a digital program.

Understand Your Market Niche and Target Audience

Knowing your market and audience isn't just about throwing a product or service out there and hoping someone buys it. If you don't know who you're serving, you'll waste time and resources chasing the wrong people. A strong business starts with a clear niche—a focused slice of the market where you can stand out.

Your **niche** is not "everyone who might need what I offer." That's too broad. Instead, it's a specific group with a shared need or problem you can solve better than anyone else. For example, instead of being a general fitness coach, you might focus on helping busy professionals lose weight without spending hours in the gym. Narrowing your niche makes your message sharper and your marketing easier because you know exactly who you're talking to.

Once you've identified your niche, go deeper. Who is your **target audience**? What do they struggle with daily? What frustrates them enough to pay for a solution? Understanding their pain points, desires, and habits is what will make your offers relevant.

Start by asking these questions:

- Who is already buying something similar to what I want to sell?
- What's missing from the current solutions?
- What would make my offer stand out to them?

Research is key. Look at competitors, read reviews, and join forums or groups where your ideal customers hang out. Pay attention to the words they use to describe their challenges—that language will help you create products, services, and marketing that resonate.

Don't worry about trying to appeal to everyone. The fastest way to be ignored is to blend in with the crowd. Instead, focus on becoming the go-to solution for one specific audience. When your business speaks directly to the right people, they notice, and they're far more likely to trust and buy from you.

Pick the model that aligns with your strengths and lifestyle. You can always adapt later, but starting with one clear path keeps your focus sharp and your strategy simple.

Define Your Unique Value Proposition (UVP)

Your Unique Value Proposition (UVP) is what makes your business stand out. It's the clear reason why someone should choose you over every other option out there. Without it, you're just another name in a crowded market, and people will default to the cheapest or most familiar option—not necessarily you.

Think of your UVP as the answer to this simple question: **Why you?** Why is your product or service the right fit for your audience's needs, and what makes it different from the alternatives? It's not about being the best at everything—it's about being the obvious choice for a specific group of people.

A strong UVP focuses on three key things:

1. **The problem you solve** – What pain or challenge are you removing for your customers?
2. **The result you deliver** – What will they gain, save, or achieve by working with you?
3. **Why you're different** – What's unique about your approach, your experience, or your offer?

Here's a quick formula to help:

"I help [specific audience] achieve [specific result] by [unique method or approach]."

For example:

"I help small business owners double their online sales by creating easy-to-manage, high-converting websites."

This is clear, direct, and tells the audience why it's worth paying attention.

To create your UVP, think about what your audience truly cares about. Are they looking to save time? Make money? Feel confident? Avoid stress? Your UVP needs to connect to their priorities, not just what you think is impressive.

Keep it short and simple—no jargon or filler. If you can't explain what makes you different in one or two sentences, you risk losing people's attention.

Your UVP isn't just for your website or pitch—it should guide everything you do, from marketing to pricing. When you know exactly why you're valuable, it becomes much easier to communicate that value to others.

Set SMART Financial and Growth Goals

If your business blueprint is the map, your goals are the checkpoints that keep you moving in the right direction. Without clear goals, it's easy to stay busy but make little real progress. That's why you need **SMART goals**—specific, measurable, achievable, relevant, and time-bound.

- **Start with Financial Goals:** How much revenue do you want to generate in the next 12 months? Break it down into smaller targets—quarterly, monthly, even weekly if needed. For example, if your goal is to earn $100,000 in a year, you know you need to hit roughly $8,300 per month. These numbers give you something concrete to aim for, rather than a vague idea of "more money."

- **Then Look at Growth Goals:** These are not just about sales but about building the structure to support your business long term. It could mean growing your audience, improving customer retention, or launching a new offer. For instance, a growth goal might be: "Build an email list of 5,000 subscribers within 12 months" or "Launch a new product by the end of Q2."

When setting goals, avoid the trap of being too broad. "I want to grow my business" doesn't tell you what success looks like. Instead, ask:

- What exactly do I want to achieve?
- How will I measure it?

- Is this realistic with my current resources?
- Why does this matter to my larger vision?
- When do I want it done?

SMART goals create focus. They also make it easier to track progress and adjust when needed. Hitting a monthly revenue target, for example, tells you your pricing and marketing are on track. Falling short means something needs tweaking.

Finally, keep your goals visible. Write them down, set reminders, and review them often. A goal you don't track is just a wish.

Outline Your 12-Month Business Action Plan

A business action plan turns ideas into steps you can follow. Without it, even the best goals stay as wishes. Think of it as your year-long game plan, broken into manageable pieces that guide your focus every month.

Start by looking at your **SMART financial and growth goals** from the previous section. What must happen in the next 12 months to achieve them? Work backward from your yearly goal. For example, if you need to hit $100,000 in revenue, break it into quarterly targets ($25,000 every 3 months) and then into monthly tasks that directly contribute to those numbers.

Your plan should include:

1. **Core milestones** – Major achievements like product launches, service rollouts, or marketing campaigns.

2. **Monthly focus areas** – The top priorities for each month (e.g., building your website, setting up email marketing, or onboarding new clients).
3. **Weekly and daily tasks** – The smaller actions that lead to your milestones, such as creating content, running ads, or networking.

Keep the plan simple. It doesn't need to be a 40-page document. A single-page roadmap with clear timelines can work better because it's easy to update and review. Overcomplicating things often leads to procrastination.

Build in regular check-ins. Review your progress every month. What's working? What's not? Do you need to adjust your pricing, marketing, or offers? Your plan is not set in stone—it's a tool that evolves with your business.

Also, include **buffer time** for unexpected challenges. Businesses rarely go exactly as planned, but with a structure in place, you can adapt without losing direction.

Finally, commit to consistency. A 12-month plan isn't about doing everything at once. It's about staying disciplined and focused on the right steps in the right order. Small, consistent actions done over time compound into the results you want.

A business blueprint isn't meant to be perfect—it's meant to give you direction. With your model chosen, audience defined, value clear, goals set, and a 12-month plan outlined, you now have a structure to follow. The next step is execution. Clarity is useless without action, and your blueprint will only work if you start putting it into motion, one step at a time.

3

Establishing a Winning Brand

Building a Brand That Resonates and Excels

Your brand is not your logo. It's not your website, your color palette, or your tagline. Those are tools. Your brand is the perception people have when they see your business name, hear about your work, or interact with your product. That perception either builds trust or pushes people away. And trust drives sales.

In a crowded market, good branding separates you from the noise. People don't just buy a product—they buy the feeling it gives them, the story behind it, and the experience attached to it. Strong branding can turn a small business into a category leader. Weak branding makes you forgettable.

This chapter is about getting intentional. You'll define how your business looks, sounds, and shows up—on every platform, in every conversation. You'll learn how to build a brand that not only looks good but connects, persuades, and sticks.

We'll start with the foundation: your brand identity.

Build a Compelling Brand Identity (Name, Visuals, Tone)

- **Start with the Name:** It needs to be easy to say, easy to remember, and easy to spell. Avoid clever names that require explanation. If someone has to ask what your name means, it's probably not doing its job.
- **Next, Visuals:** Choose a color palette that matches the tone of your business—serious or playful, premium or casual. Fonts should be readable, not trendy for trend's sake. Your logo doesn't need to be fancy—it needs to be clear and adaptable. Think of where it'll show up: social media, packaging, emails, business cards. It should work everywhere.
- **Finally, Tone:** Your brand tone is the way you "talk" to customers. Is it friendly? Bold? Professional? Humble? Pick a tone that fits your personality and audience. Then stay consistent. If your emails are casual but your website sounds robotic, it sends mixed messages.

Your identity is how people first meet your business. Make it intentional. Make it count.

Craft a Story for Your Brand that Connects Emotionally

People don't just buy products. They buy stories, meaning, and connection. Your brand story is the emotional thread that ties everything together—why your business exists, what you stand for, and how you want customers to feel when they interact with you.

A strong brand story isn't about making up a fairytale. It's about showing the real moments that shaped your business. Maybe your product solved a personal pain point. Maybe your mission comes from a family legacy or a frustration with how things are currently done in your industry. Whatever it is, it needs to feel real, relatable, and specific. Broad statements like "We care about our customers" don't land. Specific examples and moments do.

Structure your story around a simple arc: the problem, the turning point, and the solution. What challenge existed before your business came into the picture? What did you realize or experience that made you start your company? And how does your product or service make life better?

Keep the customer in mind as the silent partner in the story. You're not the hero—your customer is. Your brand is the guide. Position yourself as someone who understands their struggle and offers a better path forward.

Once you've nailed your story, use it everywhere—your About page, social media bios, pitches, packaging, even in casual conversations. Repetition builds recognition. But be consistent.

If your story is warm and personal in one place and cold and corporate in another, it breaks trust.

Finally, don't be afraid to let your story evolve. As your business grows, new chapters will naturally emerge. Let customers grow with you. Let them feel like they're part of the journey.

In short, your brand story isn't just what you say—it's what your audience remembers. Make it matter.

Develop Your Brand Voice and Consistency Across Platforms

Your brand voice is how your business sounds when it talks. It's the tone, word choice, and attitude that shows up in everything you say—emails, social posts, website copy, even customer replies.

Start by defining your tone. Are you casual or formal? Bold or soft-spoken? Direct or story-driven? Your brand voice should reflect the kind of people you want to attract. A legal firm and a streetwear brand shouldn't sound the same—and they shouldn't try to.

Once you've nailed the tone, apply it everywhere. That means your captions shouldn't sound different from your emails, and your website shouldn't feel like a different company from your blog. People trust consistency. If your voice flips from platform to platform, they'll second-guess your credibility.

Avoid the trap of switching tones just to fit trends. It might earn likes, but it damages trust if your brand starts to feel like it's playing dress-up. Be yourself. Even better—be your *business self*. Whatever you choose, stick to it.

Use simple tools to keep your voice on track: a short brand voice guide, a few dos and don'ts, and a list of common phrases or vocabulary that match your tone. If you're working with a team or freelancers, make sure everyone's on the same page.

Remember—every tweet, headline, and call-to-action adds to the overall picture people form about you. The goal is to feel familiar wherever they find you. Whether they see your post on Instagram or get a follow-up email, they should instantly know: *Yep, that's them.*

Consistency doesn't mean repeating the same message—it means speaking with the same voice. Across platforms, that's how trust gets built.

Position Your Brand for Premium Pricing

Charging more starts with showing you're worth more. If your brand looks, sounds, or behaves like a bargain option, people will expect bargain prices. But if you want to charge premium rates, your brand has to communicate premium value—visually, verbally, and operationally.

First, tighten your presentation. Your visuals need to look polished—logo, website, packaging, even your social feed. Clean design signals professionalism. Sloppy design screams discount bin.

Next, clarify what sets you apart. Premium brands don't compete on price—they compete on value, experience, or exclusivity. Maybe it's your expertise, your process, or your service level. Whatever it is, make sure it's obvious. If customers have to guess why you cost more, they won't pay it.

Language matters, too. Premium brands don't use hype or shouty copy. They're confident and calm. Speak like someone who doesn't need to beg for attention. Your tone should reflect control, not desperation.

Also, be selective about who you serve. When you try to appeal to everyone, you end up sounding generic. Premium brands speak directly to their ideal clients, not the masses. That focus helps justify your pricing.

Lastly, don't undercut yourself with discounts or inconsistent pricing. People remember the lowest price they paid. Frequent sales tell them to wait it out. Premium brands stay firm. If you do offer a discount, make sure it has a clear reason—and keep it rare.

Bottom line: People pay more when they believe they're getting more. Show that belief in how you present, position, and price yourself. Confidence, clarity, and consistency are what separate premium brands from everyone else.

Build Brand Trust Through Authenticity and Proof

People don't trust brands—they trust people. So if your brand feels fake, vague, or too polished, expect hesitation. To build real trust, you need two things: authenticity and proof. Without both, your message is just noise.

Start with authenticity. Be direct about who you are, what you do, and what you stand for. Don't exaggerate. Don't try to copy bigger brands. Don't use generic jargon to sound impressive. Just be real. If your brand is quirky, lean into that. If you're all about precision and discipline, show that. The more consistent and honest you are, the more people can connect with you.

Also, speak like a human. Ditch the corporate buzzwords. People want to know there's a real person behind the brand. That means owning your story—successes, failures, lessons learned. Share behind-the-scenes moments. Show your process. Admit when things didn't go perfectly. Vulnerability doesn't weaken your brand—it makes it relatable.

Now, pair authenticity with proof. People don't just want stories—they want evidence. This means client testimonials, case studies, screenshots of results, before-and-after comparisons, and social proof like reviews or user-generated content. The more specific the proof, the better. "We helped them increase sales" is vague. "We helped them grow revenue by 38% in 3 months" is convincing.

And yes, proof includes consistency. If you say one thing but do another, the trust breaks. Keep your promises. Respond to messages. Deliver on time. Small actions build credibility faster than big claims.

Finally, remember: trust isn't something you ask for. It's something you earn over time. Every post, email, client experience, and touchpoint either builds it or chips away at it. Stay consistent, stay honest, and always show your work.

When people believe you're real—and see the receipts—they stop questioning. They start trusting. And trust is what turns curious followers into loyal clients.

Your brand isn't just what you say—it's what people remember, repeat, and trust. By showing up with clarity, consistency, and proof, you're not just building visibility—you're building credibility. That's the difference between being seen and being chosen.

4

Mastering Marketing Magic

Strategies to Capture and Captivate Your Audience

Marketing isn't about pushing people into buying. It's about guiding them to a solution they already want—but may not know how to find. If your offer is solid and your message is clear, good marketing connects the dots. But that only happens when you choose the right tools, map the journey, and pay attention to what works.

This chapter breaks it down. No jargon. No complicated theories. Just real strategies to get the right eyes on your brand—and keep them engaged. Whether you're a solo freelancer or scaling a team, your ability to market well will decide how far your business goes.

We'll start with selecting the right channels. Then, we'll explore how to guide strangers toward becoming loyal buyers, set up systems that work even when you're offline, create content that gets clicks without being pushy, and finally, how to track the numbers that actually matter. Let's get practical.

Choose Your Marketing Channels (Organic, Paid, Social, Email, etc.)

You don't need to be everywhere—you need to be in the right places. The channels you choose will either bring clarity or chaos. Start by knowing where your audience actually hangs out. If you serve corporate clients, LinkedIn might beat Instagram. Selling visual products? Instagram and Pinterest may deliver better traction.

Organic marketing (social media, SEO, blogs) takes time but builds long-term momentum. Paid marketing (ads on Google, Facebook, etc.) gives faster results but burns cash if you don't track performance. Email still offers one of the highest returns, but only if you build and maintain a solid list.

Match your channel to your goal. Want quick traffic to a product launch? Consider paid ads. Want to grow trust over time? Use organic and email. Don't fall into the trap of spreading yourself too thin across every platform.

Pick 2–3 channels to focus on. Test, track, and improve. What works for someone else might not work for you—and that's fine. It's not about being everywhere. It's about being effective where it counts.

Understand the Customer Journey from Stranger to Buyer

Understanding the customer journey means seeing your business from your buyer's point of view—not yours. People don't land on your site or your profile and instantly buy. They move through a process. And if you don't map that process and guide them through it intentionally, you'll lose them before they ever get close to the checkout button.

It starts with awareness. At this stage, your audience doesn't know who you are or what you offer. They may not even know they have a problem that needs solving. This is where your content—blogs, videos, social posts—works to educate, entertain, and get noticed. No pitching, just value and visibility.

Next comes interest. Now they're following you or reading your emails. They're watching. Here's where you build authority and trust. Share social proof. Be consistent. Keep showing up with useful insights. You're not selling yet, but you're making it clear that you understand their challenges and have something worth paying attention to.

Then comes consideration. They start comparing solutions—yours and others. This is where clarity matters. Why you? What's your offer? How is it different or better? Don't confuse them. Make your unique value obvious. Use testimonials, case studies, free samples, or discovery calls to lower the barrier to entry.

Finally, there's the decision stage. This is the moment when the buyer either buys—or walks away. Make it easy. Make it clear. Have a smooth checkout process. Don't bombard them with last-minute doubts or pushy upsells. Reinforce the value and show that they're making a smart choice.

And here's the part many skip: after the sale is still part of the journey. Deliver what you promised. Follow up. Ask for feedback. Turn customers into advocates. A smooth post-purchase experience builds loyalty and repeat business.

If you understand this journey and design your marketing around it, you stop chasing cold leads and start building real momentum. One step at a time.

Develop Lead Magnets and Funnels

Lead magnets and funnels are how you turn attention into action.

A lead magnet is something valuable you give away for free in exchange for contact info—usually an email. It could be a PDF guide, checklist, template, quiz, mini-course, or discount code. The key is relevance. It has to solve a real problem your audience cares about, and it has to be directly tied to what you eventually want to sell. No random freebies. If you're a copywriter, don't give away a smoothie recipe.

Once someone opts in, the funnel begins. A funnel is just the step-by-step process that moves a lead toward becoming a buyer. It usually starts with an automated email sequence. That's where you build trust, show your expertise, and present your offer clearly.

Don't overcomplicate it. Your funnel doesn't need to be fancy. Just map out a logical path:

1. **Lead Magnet Delivered** – Instant value, no strings.
2. **Welcome Email** – Introduce who you are and set expectations.
3. **Education Emails** – Short, useful content that addresses common pain points or questions.
4. **Soft Pitch** – Show how your offer solves their problem.
5. **Clear Offer** – Present the product or service with urgency or incentive.

Test what works. Track open rates, clicks, and conversions. Fix weak links in the chain. And remember: one lead magnet, one goal. Don't throw in multiple calls to action. Keep it clean and focused.

The goal isn't just collecting emails—it's nurturing relationships that convert. When done right, your funnel runs in the background, warming up leads and making sales while you focus on delivering the actual service. It's your silent salesperson—and one of the most valuable systems in your business.

Create Content That Sells Without Being Salesy

Creating content that sells without sounding like a pushy car dealer is a skill—and it's essential. People don't want to be sold to. They want to be helped, understood, and respected. If your content can do that, the sale becomes a natural next step.

Start with their real problems—the stuff that keeps them up at night, not just what they say out loud. Your content should speak directly to those issues. Focus on being useful, not persuasive. Give answers, show examples, offer insights. When you do that consistently, trust builds.

Storytelling helps. Instead of just listing benefits, tell a short story about someone who struggled with a problem and found a solution—ideally your solution. People relate to people, not bullet points.

Be specific. Generic content gets ignored. Use real-world language, not buzzwords. Instead of saying "boost your productivity," say "cut your to-do list in half without missing deadlines."

Also, be human. Show your face. Share your opinions. Own your style. You don't have to be overly polished—just clear, honest, and grounded. People buy from people they feel they know.

And don't be afraid to mention your offer. Selling isn't the problem—sounding desperate is. Include your product or service naturally, like: "This is the exact process I use in my [coaching/program/service]." It's a mention, not a pitch.

Structure matters too. Make it easy to read. Short paragraphs. Clear headers. One idea per section. Guide the reader toward action without forcing it.

In short: be helpful, be real, and don't hide the fact that you have something worth paying for. If your content solves a problem, makes life easier, or saves someone time—congrats, you're already selling. You just didn't need to shout about it.

Track KPIs and Refine Campaigns for Better ROI

Tracking KPIs isn't just about numbers—it's about knowing what's working and what's wasting your time (and money). If you're running campaigns without tracking key performance indicators, you're basically flying blind.

Start by defining what success actually looks like. Is it more leads? Lower cost per click? Higher conversion rates? Don't track everything—just what matters most to your goals. Pick 3–5 metrics that give you real insight. For most campaigns, that could be cost per acquisition (CPA), click-through rate (CTR), conversion rate, and return on ad spend (ROAS).

Once your KPIs are set, monitor them regularly. Weekly is fine for most businesses. Daily if you're spending big. Use tools that make this easy—Google Analytics, Facebook Ads Manager, HubSpot, etc. Set up dashboards. Know your baseline numbers so you can spot changes fast.

But tracking alone isn't enough. You've got to adjust. If your email open rates are tanking, test new subject lines. If your landing page has traffic but no conversions, something's off—fix the copy, the layout, or the offer. Don't guess—test.

Every campaign teaches you something. Take notes. What audience performed best? Which creative drove the most clicks? Which message flopped? Use that info to tweak your next round. This is where most ROI gains come from—small, consistent improvements.

Also, kill what doesn't work. Don't sink money into a campaign out of hope or ego. Cut it, learn from it, move on.

Finally, zoom out every month. Compare KPIs across campaigns and timeframes. Are you actually improving? If not, something's broken. Better to face it early than keep pouring money into a leaky system.

Bottom line: the more you track and refine, the less you guess. And less guessing means better ROI.

5

Optimizing Sales Performance

Cultivating a Strategy for Revenue Growth

Sales isn't just about numbers. It's about people, timing, and making the right offer at the right moment. No matter how strong your product or how polished your marketing, if your sales strategy is clunky or unclear, revenue stalls. This chapter is about fixing that. It's about tightening the screws on your sales process so it doesn't leak leads or let opportunity slip through the cracks.

We're going to walk through what actually makes people say yes—starting with how buying decisions are made. Then we'll talk about crafting offers that people don't just want—they feel like they can't pass up. We'll also get into what to say and how to say it during a pitch or discovery call. The sales process can be manual, automated, or a mix of both—but it has to be consistent and scalable. And finally, we'll look at how to handle objections without getting defensive and how to close deals with clarity and confidence.

Let's start where all sales begin: inside the customer's head.

Learn the Psychology of High-Converting Sales

Sales begins long before someone clicks a button or signs a contract. It starts with a trigger—a problem they want solved or a goal they want to reach. Understanding what moves people to buy is key.

First, know that people rarely buy just for logical reasons. They may tell themselves it's about price or features, but emotion drives the decision. They want to feel smarter, safer, more capable, more respected. Your offer has to connect with that emotion, not just list specs.

Second, trust matters. Buyers have to believe that you understand their problem and that your product or service can actually fix it. That's why social proof—testimonials, case studies, referrals—still works. People want to see that others like them have taken the leap and benefited.

Finally, urgency and clarity matter. No one wants to feel pressured, but most people do need a nudge. If your offer is vague or open-ended, they'll hesitate. Make the path forward obvious and timely.

Understanding buyer psychology doesn't mean manipulating. It means respecting how people make decisions—and helping them make a good one.

Develop Your Irresistible Offers and Pricing Models

Your offer is not just a product or service—it's a solution to a real problem your customer has. If people aren't buying, chances are your offer isn't clear, valuable, or aligned with what your audience actually wants. To fix that, start by understanding the pain points you solve. What's at stake if the customer doesn't take action? What's the transformation you deliver? Your offer should speak directly to that gap.

Next, simplify the decision-making process. An irresistible offer removes friction. Include bonuses, guarantees, or limited-time incentives to make it a no-brainer. But don't go overboard. If you pile on too much, it starts to feel like you're hiding the real value behind gimmicks. Instead, lead with clarity: what they get, what it does, and why it matters.

Then there's pricing. It's not just about covering costs or undercutting the competition. Pricing signals value. If you price too low, you may seem cheap or untrustworthy. Too high without justification, and you'll scare people off. Anchor your pricing around the outcome you deliver. Think transformation, not time. And don't be afraid to tier your offers—basic, premium, and done-for-you options, for example—so you speak to buyers at different levels of readiness and budget.

Finally, test. Offers are not static. What worked last quarter might fall flat now. Pay attention to conversion rates, customer feedback, and sales patterns. Adjust your offer structure or pricing accordingly.

Your goal is to create offers that people feel foolish saying no to. Offers that solve the right problem, at the right time, for the right person. When your value is obvious, pricing becomes secondary. That's when sales start to feel less like pushing and more like inviting.

Master the Discovery Call or Pitch Process

The discovery call isn't about selling—it's about listening. If you treat it like a scripted pitch, you'll lose people. This is your chance to find out what the prospect actually needs, where they're stuck, and whether you're the right person to help.

Start by setting the tone. You're not there to pressure anyone. Let them know what the call is about, how long it will take, and what the goal is. That alone builds trust.

Then ask open-ended questions that get them talking. What's the biggest challenge they're facing? Why now? What have they tried already that didn't work? Your job here is to dig, not diagnose. Don't jump into advice mode too quickly. If you speak too soon, you might miss the real problem hiding beneath the surface.

Listen actively and take notes. Repeat their key points back to them to show you understand. When people feel heard, they're more likely to trust you. That trust is what opens the door to a real conversation about solutions.

When it's time to talk about your offer, keep it relevant. Tailor everything to what they just told you. Don't pitch a full menu of services—just present the path forward that makes the most sense based on what they need. Keep it simple. "Here's what I recommend, and here's how it works."

Then pause. Let them react. If they're in, great—move forward. If they hesitate, ask why. Is it timing? Budget? Clarity? Objections aren't personal—they're just opportunities to clarify or correct misunderstandings.

Don't force it. If they're not ready or not a fit, thank them and move on. Trying to convince the wrong person wastes your time and damages your reputation. A clean "no" is better than a drawn-out "maybe."

The goal of every discovery call isn't to close—it's to qualify. You're looking for the right person, with the right problem, at the right time. When you treat the call like a conversation instead of a sales pitch, you'll close more of the right clients and avoid the wrong ones entirely.

Build a Sales System (Automated or Manual) That Scales

To grow your business, you need a sales system that doesn't rely entirely on your time and energy. If every sale depends on you being present, you'll eventually hit a ceiling. A scalable sales system, whether automated or manual, removes that bottleneck and allows consistent, predictable revenue growth.

Start by mapping out your current sales process. What steps are required from lead to closed deal? Who's responsible at each stage? Where are leads falling through the cracks? You need to see the full picture before you can optimize or automate anything.

From there, decide how much of the system can be automated. This could include email sequences, lead qualification forms, appointment scheduling, or follow-up reminders. Tools like CRMs (e.g., HubSpot, Pipedrive, Close) make it easier to organize this flow. The goal is to remove repetitive tasks from your plate so you can focus on high-value conversations.

If you're selling high-ticket services or products, a manual system may still be necessary—especially for calls or customized offers. But even that can be structured. Use templates, scripts, and pre-call prep forms to streamline how you and your team handle sales conversations. Everyone should follow the same process to ensure a consistent experience.

As your pipeline grows, data becomes essential. Track your conversion rates at each step. Are people dropping off after the first email? Is your proposal-to-close ratio too low? This feedback tells you where to improve—whether it's better lead qualification, stronger follow-up, or clearer messaging.

Finally, document everything. A good sales system should be teachable. Whether you're hiring a sales rep or handing tasks to a VA, they should be able to step in without reinventing the will.

Bottom line: A scalable sales system frees you up to grow the business instead of chasing every lead yourself. Set it up once. Refine it over time. Then let it run.

Handle Objections Well and Close with Confidence

If you're in business, objections are part of the game. They're not rejection—they're hesitation. And hesitation is your cue to lean in, not back off.

The most common objections usually fall into a few categories: price, timing, trust, or need. "It's too expensive." "I need to think about it." "I'm not sure it'll work for me." These aren't the end of the road. They're signals that the person needs more clarity, proof, or reassurance.

The key is not to get defensive or talk over the objection. Let the person finish. Then ask follow-up questions to get to the real issue. For example, if someone says, "I need to think about it," you might ask, "What part are you still unsure about?" That opens up space for a real conversation instead of a polite goodbye.

Don't rush to discount or bend your offer. Instead, reinforce the value. Remind them of the result they want and how your solution gets them there. If they're hesitating on price, break it down into what it saves or earns them over time. If they're unsure about fit, share a relevant example or case study that speaks directly to their concern.

Confidence is key here. People buy certainty. If you sound unsure, they'll mirror that energy. But if you stay calm, listen closely, and respond with clarity, you'll guide the conversation toward resolution.

When it comes time to close, don't dance around it. Ask directly. "Is this something you want to move forward with?" or "Would you like me to send over the next steps?" Closing isn't pressure—it's leadership. You're helping them make a decision, not trapping them into one.

The better you get at handling objections, the faster you'll build trust. And the more confident you are in your close, the easier it is for the right clients to say yes. No tricks. Just clarity, calm, and knowing your value.

6

Managing Finances for Maximized Profits

Let's be honest—talking money isn't always fun, but ignoring it will strangle your business faster than any failed marketing campaign ever could. Revenue might be exciting, but profit is what keeps the lights on and the engine running. Financial discipline isn't about being stingy—it's about staying in control, especially when things get unpredictable. Whether you're landing your first client or scaling up to six figures and beyond, knowing your numbers gives you the power to make smart, confident decisions.

This chapter is about making your money work for you. No spreadsheets for the sake of spreadsheets. No gimmicky tricks. Just the core practices that help real businesses grow sustainably. We'll start by fixing the most common mistake entrepreneurs make—blending personal and business money like it's all one pot. From there, we'll talk budgeting for both stability and stretch goals. We'll get into tracking cash flow and key performance metrics, without drowning in data. We'll cover taxes, business structures, and how to avoid nasty surprises. Finally, we'll talk about how to reinvest profits—not randomly, but in ways that create lasting value.

The goal isn't to become an accountant. The goal is to build a business that's financially sound enough to survive lean seasons, smart enough to seize growth opportunities, and structured enough to protect what you've built.

Separate Personal and Business Finances

Blending personal and business finances is one of the fastest ways to mess up your books and get into trouble—both legally and operationally. Even if you're just getting started, open a separate business bank account now. It's not optional.

Keeping finances separate helps in a few critical ways. First, it gives you a clear picture of what your business is actually making and spending. If your personal grocery bill is coming out of the same account as your software subscriptions, you'll never know if your business is truly profitable. Second, it simplifies tax season. Trying to untangle personal expenses from business deductions months later is a nightmare. Third, it protects you. If your business is ever audited or sued, commingled funds can eliminate any liability protection your legal structure provides.

Separate accounts also create discipline. You'll start treating your business like a real operation, not a side hustle. That mindset shift alone is worth it. It keeps your decisions grounded in data instead of guesswork. And it gives you the ability to plan—not just hope—for financial growth.

Budget for Growth and Stability

A business without a budget is like driving blindfolded—at some point, you crash. If you want to grow, stay afloat during slow months, and avoid financial surprises, budgeting isn't optional.

Start by separating fixed and variable expenses. Fixed costs—like rent, software subscriptions, or salaries—don't fluctuate much. Variable costs—like marketing, freelance help, or shipping—change depending on activity. Knowing what's predictable and what isn't helps you prepare for lean times and capitalize during high seasons.

Next, build a monthly budget that includes all essential expenses and a buffer for the unexpected. Don't underestimate your costs, and don't overestimate revenue. Use real numbers, not hopeful guesses. Conservative projections keep you out of financial traps.

Then, define your revenue targets. Reverse-engineer your budget based on how much you need to earn to cover costs and leave a margin for growth. If you want to hire, launch a new product, or expand your services, those should be line items—not vague goals. Budgeting for growth means planning for it in black and white.

Also, create separate buckets for reinvestment. Allocate money specifically for marketing, software upgrades, team training, or other assets that help the business scale. If growth isn't in the budget, it won't happen on purpose.

Review your budget monthly. What did you actually spend vs. what you planned? Where did you go over? Where can you trim without compromising quality or momentum? It's not about cutting corners—it's about making every dollar work harder.

Finally, don't ignore cash reserves. Budget to build a safety net. Aim for at least 3–6 months of operating expenses in the bank. That buffer gives you breathing room when clients delay payments, sales dip, or the unexpected hits.

Budgeting is where your vision meets reality. It's not sexy, but it's what keeps the business alive long enough to do something remarkable. Growth without stability is a short-term win that becomes a long-term mess. Budget for both.

Track Cash Flow, Profit Margins, and Key Metrics

If you're not tracking your numbers, you're flying blind. It's that simple.

Start with cash flow. This is the real-time pulse of your business. It's the money coming in and going out. Revenue might look good on paper, but if your expenses eat it up before you even touch it, you'll find yourself in trouble. Monitor your inflows and outflows weekly, not just monthly. Use a spreadsheet, software like QuickBooks, or even a solid Google Sheet template. Know how much cash you have available at any given time.

Next, understand your profit margins. That's the percentage of each dollar you actually keep after covering costs. Gross margin shows what's left after direct costs (like materials or contractor fees), while net margin tells you what's left after everything — software subscriptions, marketing, taxes. If your margins are razor-thin, growth will be slow, and reinvestment will be hard. It may mean adjusting pricing, renegotiating vendor contracts, or cutting wasteful spending.

Key metrics vary by business, but here are some non-negotiables for most: Cost of Customer Acquisition (CCA), Customer Lifetime Value (CLV), conversion rate, average order value, retention rate, and refund rate. If you offer services, track your billable hours, project profitability, and time-to-close. If you're digital-product based, focus on sales funnel drop-offs and email open rates. Set benchmarks, monitor trends, and make adjustments based on what's moving the needle.

Don't fall into the trap of tracking data just to feel "organized." Metrics only matter if you use them. Review your numbers weekly. Ask: What's working? What's leaking? Where's the friction?

Use the data to make better decisions — not to admire it.

Bottom line: Cash flow is your fuel. Margins are your efficiency. Metrics are your dashboard. Together, they tell you if you're on the road to sustainable profit or heading straight for a crash. Keep your eyes on them. Always.

Understand Taxes and Legal Structures

If you're running a business, you need to understand how it's set up legally and how taxes will hit you. Otherwise, you're leaving yourself wide open — to the IRS, lawsuits, or just bad decisions.

Start with the legal structure. The most common options are sole proprietorship, partnership, LLC, and corporation. Each one has different rules for liability, taxes, and how you pay yourself. A sole proprietorship is the easiest to set up, but it doesn't protect your personal assets. An LLC gives you liability protection without a lot of red tape. A corporation (like an S Corp or C Corp) is more complex but may offer tax advantages, especially if you're making significant profit.

The wrong structure can cost you money or expose you to legal risk. It's worth spending a couple of hours talking to a lawyer or tax professional early on — not once the problems show up.

Now taxes. If you're freelancing or running a small operation, understand that taxes aren't withheld from your payments — you're responsible for setting that money aside. A good rule of thumb is to save 25–30% of your income for taxes. Don't spend it. Don't "borrow" from it. Just park it in a separate account.

Understand what you can write off: software, subscriptions, office expenses, a portion of your home if you work from there, marketing costs, professional services, and mileage. But don't get creative with deductions unless you're prepared to explain them in an audit. Keep clean records. Use accounting software or hire a bookkeeper — even part-time — to stay organized.

Also, be aware of self-employment tax. It's separate from income tax and hits harder than most new business owners expect. You may also need to pay estimated quarterly taxes, depending on your income level and location.

Legal structure and taxes aren't things to "figure out later." Get them right early, and you'll avoid bigger problems down the road. It's not exciting work, but it's the kind that keeps your business alive and protects your peace of mind.

Reinvest Profits Strategically to Fuel Growth

Once your business starts making a profit, the temptation is to pay yourself more or sit on the cash. But if you want real growth, you need to put that money back into the business — and do it with purpose.

Reinvesting isn't just about throwing money at random ideas. It's about identifying what will give you the biggest return — more revenue, more efficiency, or more reach. That means looking at your numbers, spotting what's working, and doubling down.

If you're a service provider, that could mean upgrading your tools or hiring someone to free up your time. If you're selling a product, it could mean boosting inventory, investing in product development, or tightening up your supply chain. If you're building a brand, it might mean pouring more into marketing or getting help with content and design to sharpen your message.

Don't blindly chase growth, though. Reinvesting needs to follow a strategy, not emotion. Don't hire because you're overwhelmed — hire because the role will generate more value than it costs. Don't spend on fancy software unless it'll directly improve speed, output, or client experience.

Track where your profit is going. Set aside a specific percentage — say 20–40% of your net profit — that's earmarked for growth initiatives. This builds the habit and gives you a clear budget. From there, you can weigh your options: new equipment, more staff, marketing campaigns, training, or even a better website.

Also, know when *not* to reinvest. If you've got debt piling up, inconsistent revenue, or no emergency savings, solve those first. Growth doesn't matter if your foundation is shaky. And reinvestment doesn't mean skipping your own paycheck forever — pay yourself a reasonable salary, then decide what extra to reinvest.

Finally, test before going all in. Try small experiments before committing to big spends. Run a short ad campaign before launching a full rebrand. Outsource a task before hiring full-time. Strategic reinvestment means learning as you go — not gambling the whole pot.

Remember: profit is not the finish line. It's fuel. Use it right, and it pushes you forward. Waste it, and you stall.

7

Transforming Obstacles into Opportunities

Running a business isn't a straight line. It's a zigzag of wins, losses, progress, and surprises. No matter how well you plan, there will be roadblocks — failed launches, bad hires, dry months, tech disasters, or client drama. The key difference between businesses that survive and those that fold isn't the size of the problem. It's how the owner responds.

Challenges are part of the game. Avoiding them isn't realistic. The goal is to spot issues early, learn from them quickly, and use them as leverage to grow stronger. This chapter will walk you through how to face problems head-on, without panic or paralysis. You'll learn to think clearly when things go sideways, recover faster, and turn the worst days into steppingstones.

Let's start with understanding where most people slip up — the common pitfalls.

Identify Common Pitfalls in Entrepreneurship

You don't have to learn every lesson the hard way. Many challenges in business follow patterns. If you know where the traps are, you can avoid a lot of unnecessary pain.

Here are the most common ones:

1. **Burnout** – Working around the clock isn't sustainable. Skipping sleep, meals, or downtime leads to mistakes, bad moods, and sloppy decisions. Rest isn't a luxury; it's a business tool.

2. **Chasing too many ideas** – Saying yes to every opportunity spreads your energy too thin. Focus on one main offer or business model until it's stable. Then expand.

3. **Ignoring the numbers** – If you're not tracking profit, expenses, cash flow, or marketing results, you're flying blind. Financial neglect is a fast track to failure.

4. **Avoiding sales** – You can't just "hope" clients come. If you don't actively market or sell, your business will stall — even if your service is amazing.

5. **Poor boundaries** – Taking on nightmare clients, saying yes to scope creep, or undercharging leads to resentment and wasted energy. Know your limits.

6. **Neglecting personal development** – Your mindset, habits, and leadership will always reflect in your business. If you grow, it grows.

Spot these patterns early. If you've already fallen into one, no shame — just fix it and move forward. Being aware of the pitfalls gives you a better shot at dodging them next time.

Build Resilience and Bounce-Back Strategies

Resilience in business isn't about pretending everything is fine. It's about staying grounded when it's not. Things will go wrong — delayed payments, failed launches, bad hires, tech issues, or life throwing curveballs.

If you're not mentally prepared, a single bad month can spiral into burnout or giving up too early.

Here's how to build real bounce-back ability:

1. **Normalize Setbacks**

   Hard days don't mean you're not cut out for this. Most businesses have dry spells, awkward pivots, and months in the red. Expect it. It doesn't mean you failed. It means you're in the process.

2. **Keep a Worst-case Plan**

   What happens if you lose a client? Or if a product flops? Have a clear backup plan. It could mean cutting back expenses, picking up a short-term freelance project, or shifting to a leaner offer. When you know what you'd do, panic loses its grip.

3. **Protect Your Energy**

    When everything feels like it's falling apart, overworking usually makes it worse. Step back. Even a half-day off can give your brain the reset it needs to think clearly and fix the problem.

4. **Focus on Small Wins**

    Don't try to solve everything in one day. Pick one action that moves the needle — follow up with a lead, launch the sales page, review expenses. Forward momentum, even tiny, builds confidence and control.

5. **Lean on Your Community**

    Isolation kills resilience. Talk to other entrepreneurs, mentors, or even a trusted friend. Not for advice — just to be seen. Most times, just knowing you're not alone can shift your mindset back into gear.

6. **Revisit Your 'Why'**

    When setbacks hit, reconnect with the reason you started. Was it freedom? Family? Impact? Let that focus ground you, especially when results aren't instant.

Resilience isn't about being tough all the time. It's about knowing how to reset, recover, and keep moving when things get hard. With a solid bounce-back strategy, setbacks won't knock you out — they'll sharpen your edge.

Learn from Failure Without Internalizing It

Failure is part of the process — not a reflection of your worth. But here's the trap: many entrepreneurs take failure personally. A bad launch becomes "I'm not cut out for this." A refund request becomes "I'm terrible at what I do." That kind of thinking will drain your confidence and slow your progress.

Here's how to learn from failure without letting it define you:

1. **Separate the Event from Your Identity**

   The launch failed — that doesn't mean *you're* a failure. The product didn't sell — that doesn't mean *you're* not good at what you do. Look at what happened without making it personal. What decision, process, or timing issue led to the result?

2. **Treat Every Failure Like Data**

   If something flops, get curious, not emotional. What worked? What didn't? What could've been clearer in the message? Did the offer match the market? This isn't about blame — it's about figuring out what to tweak next time.

3. **Write it Down, Then Move On**

   When you hit a setback, document what you learned. Bullet points. Straight to the facts. Then close the file and walk away. Don't replay the scene over and over in your head. It's handled.

4. **Share it**

   You don't have to put your lowest moments on Instagram, but talking through failures with someone who gets it can bring clarity. It removes the shame and reminds you this happens to everyone.

5. **Look for Patterns**

   One failure is data. Two or three? That's a pattern. If you keep burning out, missing sales targets, or facing client churn, dig into the root cause. That's where growth lives.

6. **Keep Building**

   The only real failure is quitting before the breakthrough. Most success stories are built on a stack of failed ideas, messy launches, and pivots that didn't work — until one did.

Failure doesn't mean stop. Learn what you need to learn, leave the rest behind, and get back to building. You're allowed to fail. You're not allowed to stay stuck there.

Adapt Your Strategy Without Abandoning Your Vision

Every entrepreneur hits a point where the original plan stops working. Sales dip, the audience shifts, or the market changes. This is when many people panic and scrap everything—

including the vision that brought them here in the first place. That's a mistake.

Your vision is your destination. Your strategy is just the route you take to get there. If the road is blocked, you don't cancel the trip—you find another way.

Adapting your strategy starts with getting honest about what's not working. If your pricing model is turning people away, change it. If your marketing isn't hitting, test new platforms or language. If your team setup is dragging things down, restructure it. But in all of that, don't lose sight of why you started this business or who you're trying to serve.

Sticking to your vision gives you consistency. It keeps your message aligned, your branding strong, and your decisions rooted. Customers pick up on that. So do investors, partners, and collaborators. If you're constantly reinventing your offer from scratch, people get confused—and confusion kills trust.

That said, staying rigid doesn't help either. The market moves fast. Consumer behavior shifts. Algorithms change. If you're not adapting, you're falling behind. The key is to stay flexible with your methods while keeping the core mission steady.

You might need to change how you deliver your product, how you sell it, or how you market it. You might pivot your niche or test a new pricing tier. That's normal. That's smart. But keep your purpose locked in. Know what problem you're solving, and why it matters.

Businesses that grow over time don't get there because they were lucky. They adapt with intention. They test and tweak and iterate, but they don't lose their identity in the process. That's what separates long-term players from short-term noise.

Adjust the route. Don't abandon the destination.

Create an Emergency Action Plan for Tough Months

Every business has slow seasons, surprise expenses, or unexpected drops in income. It's not a matter of if, but when. That's why an emergency action plan isn't optional—it's necessary. Start by identifying your non-negotiables. What are the minimum expenses you need to keep the business running? Rent, core team salaries, inventory, essential software—strip it down to the basics. This gives you a clear survival number.

Next, set aside an emergency fund. Even if it's small at first, start building it. Ideally, aim for three to six months of essential expenses. This cushion gives you room to breathe when things slow down or hit the fan.

Then outline exactly what you'll do when revenue dips. Think of it like a fire drill. You don't want to figure it out while you're in panic mode. Decide now what gets cut first—extra contractors, ad spend, new projects? Where can you tighten costs without killing momentum? Who needs to be informed, and how will you communicate changes to your team or clients?

Part of your plan should also include ways to quickly boost income. Can you offer a flash sale, a limited-time package, or revive a past service? What revenue-generating tasks can be fast-tracked when needed? Keep a short list handy so you're not scrambling for ideas under pressure. Also consider your mental game. Tough months test your mindset. Your emergency plan should include personal support—mentors, peers, or a routine that keeps your head clear.

Finally, review this plan every six months. Businesses evolve, and so do risks. Make sure your plan grows with you.

You don't need to live in fear of the slow times. But you do need to respect them. Being prepared won't stop hard months from happening, but it will keep them from turning into disasters. And most importantly, it will help you move through them with control, not chaos.

8

Shifting Your Mindset

The hardest battles aren't fought in the market—they're fought in your mind. It's not always strategy or skill that stalls progress. Sometimes, it's doubt. Fear. A loud inner critic. You can have the best offer, the sharpest plan, and still stay stuck because you haven't dealt with what's going on between your ears.

Mindset isn't just about positive thinking. It's about how you show up when things don't go as planned. It's how you handle risk, criticism, and even success. It's the mental wiring that drives your decisions, your habits, and your willingness to keep pushing.

This chapter isn't here to pump you up with motivational quotes. It's here to help you call out what's holding you back and give you practical tools to shift it. You don't need a perfect mindset. You just need one that doesn't keep pulling you off track.

Let's start by naming the fears that keep most people stuck.

Face Your Fears: Failure, Judgment, Success

Fear isn't always loud. Sometimes it hides in hesitation, procrastination, or overplanning. But whether it shows up as perfectionism or avoidance, the root is usually one of three fears: failure, judgment, or success.

Fear of failure is straightforward. It's the worry that you'll try and it won't work. That your offer will flop, your launch will bomb, or you'll waste your shot. Fear of judgment is about people. What they'll say. What they'll think. How they might see you if you mess up—or even if you do well. Then there's fear of success, which sounds backwards, but it's real. You fear what success might demand from you. Expectations, pressure, attention. A higher standard to maintain.

You don't need to eliminate fear to move forward. You need to get honest about what's driving it. Write it down. Name it. Ask yourself, "What am I really afraid of here?" Once it's out in the open, it's easier to challenge.

Fear thrives in silence. But when you face it, it loses power. You don't need to be fearless—you just need to be willing to act anyway. That's how mindset shifts begin. Not with hype, but with clarity and action.

Get Out of Your Own Way: Identify Patterns of Self-Sabotage

A lot of people blame outside forces for their slow progress—timing, market saturation, tough competition. But often, what's really in the way is them. More specifically, their patterns of self-sabotage.

Self-sabotage isn't always obvious. It can look like being "busy" without being productive. Over-researching instead of launching. Changing directions every two weeks because nothing feels "ready." Or constantly setting goals without backing them with action. It's behavior that looks logical on the surface, but underneath, it's delay. Avoidance. Fear masked as strategy.

Sometimes it comes from a fear of being seen. Other times it's rooted in perfectionism or deep imposter syndrome. You want to succeed, but part of you is afraid of what success might bring—or what failure might confirm. So instead of risking either, you stay in motion but never really move forward.

To break the pattern, you first have to notice it. Ask yourself:

- When do I pull back right before things gain momentum?
- What excuses do I fall back on when things get uncomfortable?
- What patterns repeat in my behavior that slow me down?

Don't just reflect—track it. Look at the last three months. Where did you hesitate? What did you avoid? What stories did you tell yourself to justify it?

Once you spot the pattern, name it. Then replace it. If you tend to delay launching because you want everything perfect, set a "good enough" standard and stick to it. If you freeze up when opportunities come your way, prep a go-to action plan ahead of time so you're not caught overthinking.

Self-sabotage doesn't mean you're weak or broken. It just means your brain is trying to keep you safe—often from imagined danger. You override it by acting anyway. Clarity followed by consistent action is the antidote.

You don't need to master every mindset trick. You just need to stop blocking your own progress. Once you do, everything else gets a lot easier.

Stop Playing It Safe: Embrace Risk with Wisdom

If you're building something that matters, you can't play it safe forever. Playing it safe might keep you comfortable, but it won't move you forward. Safe keeps your business small. Safe keeps your message quiet. Safe eventually becomes stuck.

But there's a difference between taking a risk and being reckless. You're not gambling blindly—you're making calculated moves. The goal isn't to avoid all risk. It's to learn how to assess risk and act anyway when the reward is worth it.

Start by looking at your default behavior. Do you wait for perfect conditions before starting something new? Do you avoid putting offers out until every detail is airtight? Do you say no to opportunities because the outcome isn't guaranteed?

That's fear dressed up as logic. Risk is part of growth. The key is learning how to minimize unnecessary damage if things don't go as planned. That means setting boundaries. Having contingency plans. Testing small before going big. But it also means knowing when you're using "planning" as a way to hide.

Every entrepreneur who grows fast takes risks. They invest in things before they feel 100% ready. They make offers before their audience is massive. They pivot when the data says it's time, not when it feels easy. They understand that sitting still is often the bigger risk.

The smartest way to embrace risk is to focus on decisions that stretch you, but don't destroy you. Spend money to buy back time. Hire before you're drowning. Launch the product before you've overthought it into oblivion. Take the leap, but have a parachute.

You'll never eliminate risk entirely—and you shouldn't try to. Risk is where momentum happens. Playing it safe is where dreams stall out.

So don't wait for full certainty. Make the move when the upside is clear, the downside is manageable, and the regret of not acting outweighs the fear of messing up. That's not reckless. That's how progress happens.

Clarify Your "Why": What Drives You Through the Grind

Running a business will test you. Some days you'll wonder if any of it is worth it. When money's tight, when nothing seems to be working, when you're exhausted—that's when your "why" matters most. Not some pretty mission statement, but a clear, personal reason that keeps you going when the work gets heavy.

Your "why" isn't about impressing anyone. It's not always deep or dramatic. Maybe you want time freedom. Maybe you're building something your kids can be proud of. Maybe you're tired of working for people who don't see your value. Whatever it is, own it. Be honest about what's really driving you.

If your only "why" is money, that's fine—just understand that money alone won't always be enough fuel when the pressure kicks in. You need something that actually connects to your values, not just your bank account. Otherwise, burnout hits fast.

Take the time to get specific. Write it down. Not just "I want to help people" or "I want freedom." Dig deeper. Why do you want those things? What will they change for you, for your family, for your future? Your "why" should be real enough to punch through the noise when you're tired or discouraged.

Clarity on this helps you say no to distractions. It helps you focus on the right kind of growth. It also keeps you grounded when things don't go to plan—because setbacks are easier to manage when you're not just chasing surface-level wins.

You don't need a perfect answer, but you do need an honest one. And you need to revisit it often. Goals will shift, seasons will change, but your core motivation should stay clear.

Know why you started. Know why you're still going. Let that drive carry you through the grind—not hype, not pressure, just purpose. That's what creates staying power.

Build Mental Habits for Confidence, Discipline, and Focus

Mindset isn't something you fix once and forget. It's a set of habits. And if you're trying to build a business, you need mental habits that keep you moving even when motivation fades—because it *will* fade.

Start with confidence. Most people think it's something you either have or don't. It's not. Confidence comes from doing hard things, repeatedly, and surviving them. It builds when you show up, even when you're unsure. So don't wait until you *feel* confident to act. Act first. The feeling follows.

Next is discipline. That's not about grinding 20 hours a day. It's about consistency—doing what matters most, even when it's boring. You'll never build anything sustainable without learning to show up on the days you don't want to. That means managing distractions, creating structure, and keeping promises to yourself. Even small ones. Especially small ones. If you can't trust your own word, momentum dies.

Then there's focus. In a world built to pull your attention in a hundred directions, focus is a weapon. Protect it. Don't confuse busyness with productivity. Pick your top priorities each day and stick to them. Set boundaries with people, with notifications, with yourself. You won't build anything meaningful if you're always chasing what's urgent instead of what's important.

These habits don't build themselves. You have to design your environment to support them. That might mean turning off your phone during work blocks. It might mean setting a regular wake-up time or scheduling breaks so burnout doesn't creep in. The structure you build *creates* the space for mental clarity.

None of this is flashy. It's not going to look impressive on Instagram. But the people who get ahead are the ones who master boring consistency. They train their mind like they train their body—reps, discipline, recovery.

Confidence. Discipline. Focus. These aren't personality traits. They're built one decision at a time. Keep choosing them until they become your default setting. That's how real progress happens—on the inside, long before the results show up on the outside.

9

Harnessing Life Insurance for Strategic Wealth Building

Most people see life insurance as a safety net—a payout for loved ones if the worst happens. While that's true, it's only part of the story. Life insurance can also be a tool for building, protecting, and transferring wealth in ways few people understand. When used strategically, it can protect your family's future *and* become an active part of your long-term financial plan.

The reality is, many high-income earners underestimate its potential because they've only been exposed to the basic "coverage" conversation. They don't realize that certain policies can act like a tax-efficient savings vehicle, a source of liquidity, and a shield for assets. Others buy policies without understanding the structure, leaving money on the table—or worse, locking themselves into something that doesn't serve their goals.

This chapter is about closing that gap. You'll learn how life insurance can be more than just a death benefit. We'll walk through the fundamentals, the mechanics of cash value growth, tax advantages, and how to use it as part of your wealth-building strategy. We'll also cover how it plays into legacy planning, so the wealth you create is protected and passed on with intention.

Integrating Protection and Prosperity

The first step to using life insurance strategically is shifting how you think about it. It's not just about replacing your income when you're gone—it's about building a financial foundation that works for you while you're still alive. Protection and prosperity don't have to be separate goals; they can be built into the same tool.

Think of protection as your financial defense. It ensures that if life takes an unexpected turn, your family, business, or estate won't be left scrambling. But prosperity—your offense—means actively growing your wealth, finding ways to make your money work harder, and keeping more of what you earn. The right life insurance policy can give you both.

For example, some policies not only pay out a death benefit but also build cash value over time. That cash value can be accessed during your lifetime—without triggering the same tax implications as other financial vehicles—if the policy is structured correctly. This means you can cover emergencies, fund opportunities, or supplement retirement income while still maintaining your coverage.

Integrating these two priorities requires understanding the type of policy that aligns with your income, goals, and time horizon. Done right, it becomes more than an expense—it becomes a cornerstone of your long-term wealth plan.

Life Insurance Fundamentals

Before using life insurance as a wealth-building tool, you need to understand the main types of policies and how they work. Each has different purposes, costs, and benefits.

- **Term Life Insurance** – This is the simplest and cheapest form. You pay premiums for a set period (10, 20, or 30 years), and if you pass away during that term, the policy pays a death benefit to your beneficiaries. It has no cash value and no investment component. Term is best for pure protection needs—like covering a mortgage or ensuring your family's income replacement—without tying up extra money.

- **Whole Life Insurance** – This is permanent coverage with fixed premiums and a guaranteed death benefit. It also builds cash value at a steady pace. The growth is slow compared to other financial vehicles, but it's predictable and tax-advantaged. Whole life is often used as a conservative, long-term asset.

- **Universal Life Insurance** – This offers more flexibility in premiums and death benefits. Cash value growth is tied to market interest rates, so returns can vary. It works for those who want more control over payments and coverage but still value permanent insurance.

- **Indexed Universal Life (IUL)** – This links cash value growth to a market index (like the S&P 500), with caps and floors to protect against losses. It offers the potential for higher returns than whole life but with more complexity. IULs are popular for those seeking a balance of growth potential and downside protection.

How It Fits into a Long-Term Strategy

Life insurance can be a defensive and offensive financial tool. It provides a guaranteed payout for protection, but certain types can also grow tax advantage cash value, offer liquidity through policy loans, and create tax-advantaged income in retirement. It's especially valuable for high earners looking to diversify and shield assets from taxes.

Beyond Coverage: An Asset Class

When structured correctly, life insurance can behave like a private savings and lending system. You can borrow against your policy for investments, business funding, or personal needs, while your cash value continues to grow.

In this way, it's not just insurance—it's a stable, tax-efficient asset in your portfolio.

Building Wealth with Cash Value

Cash value is a financial component in permanent life insurance policies such as whole life, universal life, and indexed universal life. It grows over time, often on a tax-advantage basis, and can be accessed while you're still alive.

How Cash Value Accumulates

When you pay your premium, part goes toward the cost of insurance, and part goes into the cash value account. That account earns interest or market-linked returns depending on the policy type. With whole life, the growth is at slow, but steady pace. With universal or indexed universal life, growth may fluctuate but can potentially be higher. Over time—usually after several years—cash value can become a substantial asset if the policy is funded properly.

Using Policy Loans for Liquidity

One of the most powerful features of cash value is the ability to borrow against it without triggering taxes. The insurance company lends you the money, using your cash value as collateral. You can use the funds for almost anything: business capital, real estate investments, paying off debt, or bridging income gaps. Meanwhile, your cash value continues to grow as if you hadn't touched it. Loans aren't "free"—they accrue interest—but you control the repayment terms. Many use this as a flexible source of liquidity that doesn't depend on credit checks or market conditions.

Avoiding Common Traps

The benefits only work if the policy is structured and managed correctly. Underfunding the policy in early years can stunt cash value growth. Over-borrowing without proper repayment can cause the policy to lapse, triggering unexpected taxes and eliminating your death benefit. Choosing a policy type that doesn't match your goals can also backfire—like buying an IUL for safety when you can't tolerate the variability. It's critical to work with an advisor who understands both insurance mechanics and your broader financial plan.

Cash value life insurance isn't for everyone, but for high-income earners, business owners, and disciplined savers, it can be a reliable tool for both liquidity and long-term growth—if it's set up and managed the right way.

Tax-Efficient Growth

Permanent life insurance offers a unique combination of protection and tax advantages that can strengthen your long-term wealth strategy. When structured correctly, the tax treatment of cash value growth and access can be far more favorable than many traditional investments.

Tax-Deferred Growth Benefits

Cash value grows on a tax-deferred basis, meaning you don't pay taxes on the gains each year. This allows the account to compound faster, since the money that would have gone to taxes remains invested. Over decades, the difference between taxed and tax-deferred growth can be substantial. For high-income earners who are already maxing out retirement accounts, this creates another shelter for growth without annual reporting to the IRS.

Tax Advantage Withdrawals and Loans

When it comes time to access your funds, permanent policies allow you to withdraw your original contributions (the cost basis) tax advantage. After that, you can use policy loans to tap into the remaining value without triggering taxable events. Loans aren't counted as income because you're borrowing against your own asset, not selling it. As long as the policy stays in force and is managed properly, this money can be accessed without income taxes. This makes life insurance one of the few vehicles where you can grow money tax-deferred and later access it without tax erosion.

Using Life Insurance to Shield Wealth

In addition to income tax benefits, many states provide creditor protection for the cash value and death benefit in a life insurance policy. This means your money may be shielded from lawsuits or claims, depending on state law. For business owners and professionals in high-liability fields, this protection can be a valuable layer of financial defense. Combined with the death benefit, it ensures that both you and your heirs can retain more of your wealth instead of losing it to taxes or legal judgments.

When integrated into a broader plan, life insurance can act as both a growth engine and a tax advantage. The key is proper funding, disciplined borrowing, and regular policy reviews to avoid unexpected tax consequences.

Legacy and Estate Planning

Life insurance isn't just about protecting income—it's also one of the most efficient tools for passing wealth to the next generation. When structured correctly, it can help you transfer assets tax-efficiently, preserve family wealth, and create an intentional financial legacy.

Leaving Behind Generational Wealth

The death benefit from a permanent life insurance policy is generally paid to beneficiaries income-tax-free. This provides an immediate, liquid asset that can cover final expenses, replace lost income, and fund long-term goals for your heirs. For many, this becomes a foundation for generational wealth—money that can be used for education, starting businesses, buying property, or investing. Because the payout is guaranteed as long as premiums are maintained, it offers certainty that other investments can't match.

Minimizing Estate Taxes

For larger estates, federal and state estate taxes can erode what's left for heirs. Life insurance can be used to offset these taxes or reduce their impact. One common strategy is placing the policy inside an Irrevocable Life Insurance Trust (ILIT), which keeps the death benefit outside of your taxable estate. This allows you to pass on the full value of the policy without it counting toward estate tax thresholds. In cases where taxes are unavoidable, the death benefit can provide the liquidity needed to pay them without forcing heirs to sell property or other assets quickly.

Creating a Financial Legacy with Intention

A policy's death benefit can be directed according to your values and goals. You can structure payouts to support specific causes, create scholarships, or fund charitable organizations through a charitable remainder trust.

You can also set conditions for how and when heirs receive funds—such as staggered payments at certain ages or for specific purposes—to ensure the money is used wisely. This intentional planning helps protect your legacy from being diminished through poor financial decisions or disputes.

When combined with other estate planning tools, life insurance offers control, protection, and efficiency. It's not just about leaving money—it's about making sure that money accomplishes what you want it to, long after you're gone.

Real-World Application

<u>Case Studies of Six-Figure Earners Using Life Insurance</u>

High-income earners often face two challenges—higher taxes and the risk of losing wealth through poor planning. For example, a 42-year-old consultant earning $250K annually used an indexed universal life policy to allocate part of her bonus income. Over 15 years, her cash value grew with tax advantages, allowing her to take policy loans for real estate down payments without triggering taxable events. Another example is a business owner who used whole life insurance as collateral for a business expansion, avoiding traditional bank financing and keeping interest payments inside his own policy. Both cases show how strategic policy use can support growth while protecting assets.

Worksheets, Tools, and Action Steps

To apply these strategies, start with three key steps:

1. **Run the Numbers** – Use a cash flow worksheet to identify how much you can allocate to premiums without straining your budget.

2. **Define Your Objectives** – Rank your priorities: wealth growth, tax advantages, estate planning, or liquidity.

3. **Model Different Scenarios** – Work with an advisor or use an online policy illustration tool to project performance under various funding schedules.

Having these details in writing will make your conversations with advisors far more productive.

How to Choose the Right Advisor and Structure

Not all financial professionals understand how to optimize life insurance for wealth-building. Look for an advisor who:

- Specializes in advanced insurance planning, not just selling policies.
- Can explain policy mechanics without jargon.
- Shows you multiple funding and structure options, with transparent illustrations.
- Understands tax implications and works alongside your CPA or estate attorney.

For high earners, policy structure is critical. Overfunding the policy early (while staying under IRS limits to avoid Modified Endowment Contract status) can significantly boost cash value growth. Using riders like waiver of premium or overloan protection can help safeguard the policy long-term.

By applying tested strategies, tracking your own numbers, and working with the right professional, life insurance shifts from being just "coverage" to becoming a flexible financial tool that supports growth, liquidity, and legacy—without leaving opportunity on the table.

When structured and managed correctly, life insurance can be more than a safety net—it can be a strategic tool for growth, liquidity, and legacy. The key is working with the right advisor, funding it properly, and using it intentionally to align with your long-term financial plan.

10

Systems and Automation for Scalable Success

Free Your Time, Scale Your Impact

If you want to grow without burning out, systems and automation are non-negotiable. Automation is not about replacing people; it's about removing repetitive work so you can focus on decisions that move the business forward. Systems create consistency, reduce errors, and make growth predictable. This chapter shows you how to pick the right tools, automate the right tasks, and set up reliable processes so your business runs whether you're at your desk or not.

We'll cover how to identify what should be automated, choose tools that fit your model, delegate effectively, write standard operating procedures, and create space to work on the business rather than in it.

The goal is practical: free your time, protect your revenue streams, and scale impact without sacrificing quality.

Identify What to Automate: Marketing, Sales, Customer Onboarding

Start by mapping tasks across marketing, sales, and onboarding. Not everything needs automation. Use a simple priority test: task frequency, time cost, error risk, and impact on revenue. High-frequency, low-complexity tasks with high time cost are the best candidates.

In marketing, automate lead capture and follow-up sequences. Set up landing pages, opt-in forms, and email workflows that deliver lead magnets and nurture prospects. Schedule social posts, but reserve high-touch content for manual posting. Use basic ad rules to pause poor performing creatives and scale winners. Automate reporting so you get weekly dashboards without digging through platforms.

For sales, automate qualification and scheduling. Use pre-qualification forms or chatbots to filter leads, then let scheduling tools handle calendar invites.

Send templated proposals and contracts automatically once a lead hits a qualification threshold. Keep personalized outreach for high-value opportunities; automation should handle the repetitive tasks that waste time.

Customer onboarding benefits hugely from automation. Deliver welcome emails, onboarding checklists, video tutorials, and setup reminders via automated sequences. Use trigger-based workflows to push clients to the next step and to alert a human when hands-on support is needed. Automate recurring billing, invoicing, and basic support tickets to maintain cash flow and reduce friction.

Always pair automation with clear SOPs and monitoring. Build in human checkpoints, measure results, and iterate. Start small, prove value, then expand. Automation is a tool—used well, it frees your time; used poorly, it creates silent failures. Treat automation like an investment: measure outcomes, control risk, and reinvest time savings into strategic growth and leadership.

Choose Tools and Platforms That Fit Your Business Model

The wrong tool can slow you down more than doing the task manually. The right one integrates smoothly with your workflow, supports your goals, and scales as you grow. Choosing tools isn't about finding the most advanced option; it's about finding the one that matches how your business operates.

Start with your business model. Are you service-based, product-based, subscription-driven, or a hybrid? A coaching business might prioritize scheduling and video conferencing tools. An e-commerce store needs strong inventory management and payment processing. A subscription model benefits from recurring billing systems and churn analytics. Match the tool's core strength to your main revenue driver.

Next, define your non-negotiables. This includes must-have features, security requirements, compliance needs, and integration with your existing stack. If your CRM can't sync with your email platform or accounting software, it creates bottlenecks. Look for tools with open APIs or native integrations to keep workflows connected.

Ease of use matters. A powerful platform that your team struggles to operate will cost more in training and mistakes than it saves in efficiency. Test usability with real workflows before committing. Many platforms offer free trials—use them to run a small project and measure time saved, error reduction, or conversion improvements.

Scalability is another key factor. A tool that works for a business of 10 clients may not work for 1,000. Check if the platform can handle increased volume without a major migration later. Also, evaluate the cost structure—some tools become expensive as you scale, which can eat into margins.

Support and reliability are critical. Downtime or poor support during an issue can cost revenue and damage client relationships. Choose vendors with strong customer service and documented uptime.

Finally, avoid the trap of over-stacking. Too many tools create complexity, data silos, and higher costs. Audit your stack twice a year to remove redundant platforms. Aim for a lean, integrated system where each tool has a clear purpose and delivers measurable results.

The goal isn't to chase trends—it's to build a toolset that strengthens your core processes, supports growth, and frees your team from repetitive work so they can focus on high-value activities.

Delegate, Outsource, or Eliminate Repetitive Tasks

Your time is limited. Every hour spent on low-value, repetitive work is an hour not spent on strategy, growth, or client relationships. The fastest path to scale is to remove yourself from as many operational tasks as possible. That starts with deciding whether a task should be delegated, outsourced, or eliminated altogether.

Begin by auditing your weekly activities. Track every task for one to two weeks, then sort them into three categories: must be done by you, could be done by someone else, or doesn't need to be done at all. Be honest—many tasks feel important because they're familiar, not because they drive results.

Delegation applies to tasks that need to stay in-house but don't require your direct involvement. This could include client follow-ups, document preparation, scheduling, or routine reporting.

Assign these to a team member with clear instructions and measurable expectations. Build a system so the work gets done consistently without your oversight.

Outsourcing works for specialized tasks or overflow work where hiring full-time isn't necessary. For example, a business owner might outsource graphic design, bookkeeping, paid ad management, or customer service overflow to freelancers or agencies. The advantage is flexibility—you pay for the work when you need it, without long-term payroll costs.

Elimination is often overlooked but just as powerful. Some tasks exist out of habit or outdated processes. If a report is never reviewed, stop generating it. If a meeting doesn't lead to decisions or action, remove it from the schedule. Each task eliminated frees time and mental space for higher-value work.

To make this sustainable, document standard operating procedures (SOPs) for tasks you delegate or outsource. This ensures consistency and allows new team members or contractors to step in without long training periods. The goal is to position yourself where your time delivers the highest return—usually in strategic decision-making, relationship-building, and revenue generation. Every repetitive task you hand off or remove moves you closer to running the business rather than being trapped inside it.

Scaling isn't just about doing more—it's about doing less of the wrong things and ensuring the right things get done by the right people or systems.

Build SOPs (Standard Operating Procedures) for Consistency

Scaling a business requires consistency. Without it, quality drops, mistakes increase, and clients lose trust. Standard Operating Procedures (SOPs) are the solution. They're step-by-step instructions for how tasks should be completed, ensuring the same result every time—regardless of who's doing the work.

Start by identifying the tasks that happen most often in your business—client onboarding, invoicing, order fulfillment, marketing campaigns, or customer support processes. These are prime candidates for SOPs because they're repeated regularly and impact customer experience.

Each SOP should clearly outline:

1. **Purpose** – Why the task matters and what it achieves.
2. **Scope** – Where it applies and any limitations.
3. **Step-by-step instructions** – Detailed enough that someone new can follow without guessing.
4. **Tools and resources** – Links, templates, or login details needed to complete the task.
5. **Quality checks** – How to confirm it's been done correctly.

Keep SOPs simple and easy to access. Overcomplicating them defeats the purpose. Use plain language, bullet points, and visuals where possible. Store them in a shared drive, project management tool, or SOP software so everyone can find and use them quickly.

Once an SOP is written, test it by having someone unfamiliar with the process follow it. If they can complete the task without asking questions, it's clear enough. If not, refine it.

SOPs also make delegation and outsourcing easier. Instead of spending hours training someone verbally, you hand them the document and have them follow the process. This shortens onboarding time and ensures consistent results from day one.

Another benefit—SOPs protect your business from dependency on one person's memory or skills. If a team member leaves, the process doesn't leave with them. Anyone can step in and keep things running smoothly.

Review SOPs regularly. Technology changes, tools update, and your business evolves. Outdated procedures create confusion and errors. Schedule quarterly or biannual reviews to keep them relevant.

The bottom line—SOPs remove guesswork, reduce errors, and make your operations scalable. They free you to focus on growth, knowing the day-to-day runs like clockwork. In a scaling business, that kind of consistency isn't just helpful—it's non-negotiable.

Create Freedom: Work ON Your Business, Not IN it

The ultimate goal of building systems and automating processes is to create freedom—time, mental space, and energy—to focus on the bigger picture. Many business owners get stuck working in their business, doing daily tasks that keep things running but prevent growth. To scale, you need to shift to working on your business.

Working in your business means you're handling client calls, sending invoices, troubleshooting tech issues, or managing day-to-day operations. These tasks are important, but they're not where your highest value lies. Working on your business means you're setting strategy, building partnerships, creating new offers, and looking for ways to improve and expand. It's about steering the ship, not rowing it.

This shift only happens if you have systems, automation, and delegation in place. Without them, you'll always be tied up in the small tasks that someone else—or something else—could handle. The goal is to design operations so they can run without you being involved in every detail.

Start by asking yourself: If I stepped away for a month, could the business still run smoothly? If the answer is no, find the gaps. That could mean documenting processes, hiring support, or automating repetitive workflows.

Once the basics are handled by people and systems you trust, you can focus on higher-value activities. This might mean developing long-term growth plans, identifying new markets, strengthening your brand, or improving customer experience at a strategic level.

Creating freedom also means protecting your time. Block out portions of your schedule for planning, creative work, and big-picture thinking. Treat these as non-negotiable. Avoid being pulled back into operational work unless absolutely necessary.

The payoff of this shift is twofold: your business grows faster, and your quality of life improves. You're no longer exhausted from putting out fires all day. Instead, you're guiding the vision, shaping the future, and making decisions that have a lasting impact.

Working on your business instead of in it is the difference between being self-employed and being a true business owner.

One keeps you busy; the other keeps you free. And freedom is what makes scaling sustainable.

Scaling successfully isn't about doing more—it's about doing less of the wrong things and more of the right ones. By automating key processes, choosing the right tools, delegating effectively, documenting workflows, and protecting your time, you build a business that runs smoothly without constant oversight. This frees you to focus on growth, innovation, and impact—the work only you can do. The systems you put in place today are what make long-term freedom and sustainable success possible.

11

Expanding Your Influence and Network

Level Up Through Strategic Relationships

Influence is rarely built in isolation. The leaders who make the greatest impact understand that relationships are the true currency of growth. Skills, ideas, and vision matter, but they reach their full potential only when they are connected to the right people. Expanding your network is not about collecting business cards or social media followers—it's about deliberately aligning yourself with individuals and groups who can sharpen your thinking, open new doors, and amplify your results.

When your network grows with purpose, your opportunities multiply. You find mentors who have already walked the path you're on, collaborators who share your goals, and communities that keep you accountable. These connections create a multiplier effect—your influence expands because you're plugged into people who already have reach, credibility, and resources.

At this stage in your leadership journey, your focus shifts from simply managing your own work to creating a platform that others can stand on with you. This is how you elevate your authority, accelerate your revenue, and sustain momentum over time. Every strategic connection you make either strengthens your foundation or extends your reach. The key is knowing which relationships deserve your investment and how to cultivate them.

Grow Your Circle: Mentors, Masterminds, and Collaborators

First, know the role each plays. A mentor provides perspective and experience. A mastermind is a peer group that gives feedback and accountability. A collaborator is someone who complements your skills to produce work or open markets.

Identify gaps before you reach out. What skill, connection, or perspective do you lack? Be precise—"I need help with scaling paid ads" is stronger than "I need marketing advice." Use that clarity to find the right person.

Where to find them: industry events, niche online communities, LinkedIn with targeted searches, referrals from people you already trust, and curated mastermind programs. For mentors, prioritize people who've done what you want to do and who show a willingness to teach. For masterminds, look for mixed expertise, similar ambition, and a track record of accountability. For collaborators, find complementary skills and aligned work ethics.

When you reach out, be direct. Say who you are, what you're building, what you need, and what you offer in return. Ask for a short call—don't demand a long commitment up front. Respect their time.

Structure matters. For mentors, set a cadence (monthly or quarterly), prepare questions in advance, and deliver updates so they see progress. For masterminds, agree on size, frequency, confidentiality, and a simple agenda that returns value to every member. For collaborators, use a clear scope, timeline, deliverables, and written terms—clarity prevents friction.

Keep the relationship alive by delivering value: share introductions, insights, or help when you can. Show up on time, follow through, and be specific about outcomes. Over time, these relationships compound—small, consistent investments in other people pay off far more than random networking.

Use Social Proof and Media to Elevate Your Authority

People trust what other people validate. Social proof is one of the fastest ways to build credibility because it shows that others have tested, experienced, and endorsed what you offer. When you position those endorsements strategically, you stop being another voice in the crowd and start becoming a trusted authority.

Social proof can take many forms: client testimonials, case studies, reviews, media features, speaking engagements, or high-profile collaborations. The key is to choose formats that speak directly to your target audience. A CEO deciding whether to hire you will value a feature in a respected industry journal more than a string of casual Facebook comments. A small-business owner might respond better to a relatable client success story than to a corporate press release.

Start with what you already have. Pull together positive client feedback, measurable results you've delivered, and notable partnerships. Package these in a way that is easy to understand—short, specific, and relevant. For example, "We increased their conversion rate by 42% in three months" says far more than "We helped their business grow."

Media can extend your reach beyond your immediate network. Guest articles, podcast interviews, industry panels, or local news features position you in front of audiences you couldn't reach alone. Being quoted as an expert gives you third-party validation that advertising cannot buy.

Don't wait for opportunities to come to you—pitch them. Research media outlets, podcasts, or event organizers whose audiences align with yours. Craft a clear, relevant pitch that explains the value you'll bring to their audience. Over time, consistent visibility will make you the go-to choice in your space.

Finally, make your social proof easy to find. Feature it on your website, weave it into presentations, highlight it on social media, and include it in proposals. The more people see others vouching for your work, the faster they'll decide to trust you.

Social proof and media coverage aren't just about attention—they're about leverage. They allow you to step into bigger conversations, command higher fees, and open doors that cold outreach rarely unlocks. When others speak well of you, your authority grows without you having to say a word.

Learn the art of positioning yourself as a thought leader

Positioning yourself as a thought leader is about being intentional with how you present your ideas, expertise, and experiences so they stand out in a crowded space. It's not just sharing what you know—it's sharing it in a way that makes people see you as a trusted authority whose perspective is worth seeking out. This means curating your content, speaking opportunities, and public presence so that they align with a clear, consistent message.

Start by defining your area of expertise and the unique lens you bring to it. Thought leaders aren't generalists—they're known for having a strong, clear point of view in a specific domain. Once you know what that is, make sure every article you write, podcast you appear on, and presentation you deliver reinforces that positioning. Over time, repetition of a focused message builds recognition.

Next, engage in conversations that matter. This could mean contributing to industry panels, writing guest columns for respected publications, or participating in high-level forums where your peers and audience are paying attention. The goal is to be part of shaping the conversation, not just reacting to it.

Show that you have both depth of knowledge and the ability to connect it to broader trends and challenges.

Your digital footprint is equally important. When someone Googles your name, they should see a body of work that reflects authority and thoughtfulness. Publish well-researched articles, post insightful commentary on relevant issues, and share original perspectives that add value. Consistency here is key—sporadic posting won't build momentum.

Finally, credibility grows when others cite, quote, or reference your work. This comes from building relationships with other influencers, journalists, and leaders in your space. When your ideas are shared or discussed by respected voices, your authority compounds. Positioning yourself as a thought leader is a long-term process, but every article, talk, or interview becomes another brick in the foundation.

Done right, this positioning shifts how opportunities find you. Instead of chasing speaking gigs, partnerships, or media coverage, you start attracting them. You become the go-to name in your area, not because you said you were an expert, but because the market has decided you are one.

Build Partnerships that Accelerate Your Revenue

Partnerships can move your revenue forward faster than almost any solo effort. The right partner brings access to audiences, resources, and credibility that would take years to build on your own. The wrong partner can slow you down or damage your brand. The key is to be intentional in choosing relationships that align with your goals and deliver measurable value.

Start by identifying gaps in your current business model. Do you need more exposure? A stronger distribution channel? Additional expertise? Look for partners who can fill those gaps and for whom you can provide equal value in return. This mutual benefit is what makes partnerships sustainable.

Approach potential partners with a clear proposal. Show them exactly how working with you will help them reach their own objectives—whether that's increased visibility, expanded offerings, or access to a new market. Avoid vague ideas about "collaboration" and instead present defined outcomes and timelines.

Revenue-focused partnerships often take the form of co-branded products, joint marketing campaigns, affiliate relationships, or bundled services. For example, a business coach could team up with a marketing agency to offer a combined program. Both parties tap into each other's client base, share promotional costs, and split the resulting revenue.

Once a partnership is formed, set clear agreements from the start. Define deliverables, responsibilities, timelines, and how revenue will be shared. This prevents misunderstandings and keeps both sides accountable. If possible, put these agreements in writing to avoid disputes later.

Monitor the results closely. If a partnership is driving strong revenue growth, invest more resources into it. If it's underperforming, identify the problem quickly and either adjust the approach or move on. Partnerships work best when there's ongoing communication and a willingness to adapt strategies.

The most effective revenue partnerships also go beyond one-off transactions. They develop into long-term alliances where both parties actively look for new ways to help each other grow. This trust and continuity create a compounding effect on revenue over time.

When you align with the right partners, you gain more than just sales—you gain momentum. Instead of pushing your business forward alone, you have multiple forces pulling in the same direction. That kind of acceleration is hard to match with any other growth strategy.

Give Value First, Grow Through Contribution

When you lead with value, you build trust faster than any pitch can. People naturally gravitate toward those who help them solve problems, open doors, or share insights without expecting an immediate return. This approach shifts you from being just another professional trying to sell something into someone whose presence is genuinely beneficial. That shift changes how others engage with you—conversations become warmer, and opportunities emerge without you having to chase them.

Giving value first can take many forms. You might share a resource that saves someone time, introduce them to a contact who can advance their work, or provide expertise that helps them avoid a costly mistake. It doesn't have to be grand or expensive—what matters is that it's relevant and genuinely useful. The goal is to create a pattern where people associate your name with progress, clarity, or opportunity.

This approach works best when you're consistent. One act of generosity might be appreciated, but repeated acts build a reputation. Over time, people begin to see you as someone who lifts others up, which attracts collaborators, clients, and partners who want to work with people they trust. The return on this mindset often comes indirectly. Someone you helped six months ago may later refer you to a major opportunity. A peer you supported early in their career may become a key decision-maker and remember your contribution.

Importantly, giving value first doesn't mean being a doormat or giving away the core of your business for free. Boundaries matter. The art is in knowing what to give freely to build goodwill and what to reserve for paid engagements. A well-chosen piece of advice, a shared framework, or a connection to the right person can be worth far more than a cold sales pitch.

Growing through contribution also changes how you see your network. Instead of viewing it as a list of potential buyers, you start to see it as an ecosystem—one that thrives when you help it grow. When you operate this way, your own success becomes linked to the success of others, creating a cycle where everyone benefits. The result is growth that's sustainable, not just in revenue, but in influence, credibility, and long-term opportunity.

Partnerships and contribution are long games. They're built on a steady rhythm of showing up, following through, and keeping your word when it's least convenient. Whether you're connecting with mentors, collaborating with peers, or adding value without an immediate return, every action plants seeds. Some will grow fast, others will take time—but all of them strengthen your network and reputation. Keep your focus on building trust and creating impact, and you'll find that opportunities have a way of finding their way back to you.

12

Living the Six-Figure Lifestyle (without Burnout)

Sustainability, Fulfillment, and Long-Term Vision

Most people inherit their definition of success without ever realizing it. It's absorbed from parents, culture, industry norms, or the loudest voices in the room. By the time you start chasing it, the measure of "making it" may already be set—bigger title, larger paycheck, more visibility. But when you stop and question where that target came from, the answer can be unsettling. Was this the life you wanted, or the life you were told to want?

Success, in its most useful form, is deeply personal. It's the alignment between what you value and how you live. The trap is when you measure it only in external terms—income, recognition, or material wins—while ignoring whether you actually enjoy the process of getting there or living there. Leaders, especially, can be pulled into this external scorekeeping. You spend years building a career only to arrive at a peak that feels hollow. The résumé looks impressive; the reality feels disconnected.

This chapter is about turning the lens inward before chasing the next milestone. It's about defining what success means in a way that's durable, meaningful, and sustainable—so you're not just achieving more, but living better.

Define What Success Feels Like—Not Just What It Earns

A balanced definition of success starts with the feeling it gives you, not the rewards it hands you. That doesn't mean ignoring outcomes—it means anchoring them to something more enduring than a bank balance or job title.

Think about the moments in your work when you've felt at your best. Not the flash of recognition after an award, but the steady satisfaction of doing something that mattered, using skills you enjoy, with people you respect. Those experiences create a kind of internal wealth that outlasts external measures. The challenge is they're easy to overlook because they don't come with a certificate or a headline.

When you define success only by what it earns, you risk building a life that looks good on paper but feels like a constant trade-off. The financial gains and professional wins are real, but they may come at the cost of health, relationships, or personal fulfillment. Over time, that imbalance shows up as burnout, disconnection, or the sense that you're running hard without moving closer to anything you actually want.

Defining what success feels like starts with a clear inventory of your values and non-negotiables. Ask yourself:

- What kind of work makes me feel energized instead of drained?
- Who do I want to be when I'm at my best?
- What am I unwilling to sacrifice—even for a significant reward?

The answers might surprise you. They often reveal that the best version of success is simpler and more within reach than the one you've been chasing. For some, it's flexibility. For others, it's building something lasting. For many, it's the ability to finish a day's work proud of the way it was done.

When you define success this way, the external rewards still matter—but they stop being the whole story. You're no longer measuring your worth by numbers alone, but by the quality of the life those numbers help you create. That shift changes the way you make decisions, what opportunities you accept, and how you handle setbacks. It keeps you from chasing a version of success that might look impressive from the outside but feels empty once you arrive.

Time Management for Energy, Health, and Joy

Time management isn't just about squeezing more into your day. It's about protecting the quality of your hours so they serve your goals—and your life—without draining you. You can hit every deadline and still be burnt out if you manage your schedule purely for productivity. The real aim is to align your time with your energy rhythms, health needs, and the things that make life worth living.

Start by mapping your natural energy curve. Pay attention for a week to when you feel most focused, most creative, and most tired. Protect those high-energy windows for your most demanding work. If your mind is sharpest in the morning, that's when you should tackle strategy, problem-solving, or writing—not emails or admin work. Low-energy periods are better suited to routine tasks. By matching the type of work to the right part of your energy cycle, you'll get more done with less strain.

Guard your health by treating breaks and rest as non-negotiable. Many people think of downtime as a luxury, but it's the reset that keeps your output steady and your mind sharp. Schedule breaks before you crash. Even a five-minute walk or some deep breathing can clear mental clutter. Longer breaks—like lunch away from your desk or an afternoon reset—can prevent the slow creep of exhaustion.

Your calendar should reflect more than just work. Block time for movement, healthy meals, and the relationships that give you joy. If you wait to "find time" for them, they'll be the first to go when work gets busy. That imbalance might not show in a week, but it will over months or years. Success that sacrifices your health and happiness isn't really success—it's deferred burnout.

Be intentional about saying yes. Every commitment takes a piece of your energy. Before agreeing to something, consider not only the time it will take but the energy it will cost. The same hour can feel light or heavy depending on what it demands from you. Choose accordingly.

Finally, give your time structure but not rigidity. Plans keep you on track, but life will throw interruptions, surprises, and opportunities your way. Leave buffer space so adjustments don't derail you.

The way you manage your time shapes the quality of your life. Aim for a calendar that supports your energy, sustains your health, and makes room for joy—not one that simply proves you can keep busy.

Avoid the Trap of Hustle Culture—Balance Ambition with Wellness

Hustle culture sells the illusion that nonstop work equals success. In reality, it often leads to exhaustion, strained relationships, and declining performance. There's a difference between working hard and working yourself into the ground. Leaders who push themselves to the edge may get short-term wins, but they eventually pay for it in burnout, poor decision-making, and missed opportunities to recharge and think strategically.

Ambition is important. But ambition without boundaries becomes self-sabotage. The most effective leaders pace themselves, treating energy like a valuable resource. They work with intensity when it's needed and step back to recover before fatigue turns into a crisis. That balance isn't weakness—it's sustainability.

This starts with setting clear, realistic priorities. Not everything is urgent. Not every opportunity is worth pursuing. Ask yourself: Which tasks truly move the needle toward my goals? Which can be delegated, delayed, or dropped? Every "yes" you give to something low-value steals time and mental bandwidth from what actually matters.

Wellness isn't just about exercise or nutrition—it's about protecting your ability to show up as your best self over the long haul. That means carving out space for rest, hobbies, family, and mental clarity. Think of it as strategic downtime: the moments when your body and mind recharge so you can return sharper and more focused.

Boundaries are essential. Communicate them clearly to your team and stick to them yourself. If you model being available 24/7, your team will think that's the standard. On the other hand, if you demonstrate disciplined work hours, they'll see that excellence doesn't require constant grind.

Finally, don't confuse movement with progress. Many people in hustle culture stay busy to feel productive, but they aren't actually advancing their goals. Measure your days by outcomes, not hours worked. Create systems that deliver results without relying on constant personal effort, so you're not trapped in an endless work loop.

Balanced ambition creates leaders who last. When you align your drive with sustainable habits, you gain the endurance to lead for years instead of burning out in months. The real game is staying sharp, healthy, and energized—so you can keep winning without losing yourself in the process.

Plan for Long-term Wealth: Retirement, Investments, and Passive Income

Long-term wealth doesn't happen by accident. It requires clear goals, consistent action, and a willingness to think beyond immediate gains. The first step is to define what financial security means for you—not just in numbers, but in the lifestyle and choices you want decades from now. That clarity guides every decision you make today.

Retirement planning starts with understanding how much you'll need and when you'll need it. Relying solely on a pension or social security is risky. Build personal savings and investment accounts that grow over time. Use tax-advantaged vehicles like retirement funds to maximize compounding and reduce unnecessary losses to taxes. The earlier you start, the less you'll need to contribute each month to reach your goals.

Investments should be diversified across assets that match your risk tolerance and timeline. This might include stocks for growth, bonds for stability, real estate for tangible value, or index funds for broad market exposure. Avoid putting everything into one "hot" idea or relying on short-term speculation. Sustainable wealth is built on steady returns, not gambling.

Passive income adds another layer of security. This could come from rental properties, dividend-paying stocks, royalties from creative work, or business systems that generate revenue without constant input. The aim is to create streams of income that keep flowing whether you're working or not, reducing the pressure to trade time for money.

Regularly review your financial plan and adjust it as life changes. Income fluctuations, market shifts, and personal priorities all affect your strategy. What worked five years ago may not work now. The point is to stay engaged with your money, not to set a plan and forget it.

Finally, protect your wealth. Insurance, legal safeguards, and an emergency fund are all part of ensuring that one setback doesn't undo years of progress. Wealth is as much about defense as it is about growth.

Long-term financial health frees you to make choices from a position of strength. It means you can say yes to opportunities and no to demands that don't serve you, because your future is already accounted for. That's not just money in the bank—it's peace of mind.

Celebrate Wins and Keep Evolving the Vision

Celebrating wins is more than an emotional boost—it's a strategic move. When you pause to acknowledge progress, you create momentum. Wins, big or small, signal that your actions are working. They validate the effort, sharpen your confidence, and give your team or partners a reason to stay engaged. If you skip this step and only focus on what's next, you risk burnout and a culture where progress goes unnoticed.

Celebration doesn't have to mean throwing a big party every time you hit a goal. It can be as simple as taking a moment to acknowledge the milestone in a team meeting, sending a personal thank-you to someone who contributed, or privately reflecting on what went right. The key is to be intentional. Recognize the effort behind the outcome, not just the result itself.

At the same time, wins are checkpoints, not finish lines. They should prompt you to ask: *Where do we go from here?* A business or career built for the long haul is in constant motion. Success in one area often exposes new opportunities—or reveals weaknesses that were hidden before. By treating every win as both a victory and a learning moment, you stay adaptable.

Evolving your vision isn't about abandoning what's worked; it's about refining and expanding it. The market changes, technology shifts, and personal priorities evolve over time. A static vision eventually becomes outdated. Review it regularly and adjust based on real data, current goals, and lessons learned from both your successes and failures. This doesn't mean making impulsive changes—it's about staying aligned with reality while keeping your ambitions alive.

Balancing celebration with evolution keeps you grounded yet forward-looking. You appreciate how far you've come, but you're never so comfortable that you stop pushing forward. It's a rhythm: achieve, celebrate, reassess, and move. Leaders who master this rhythm create resilience in themselves and their teams. They avoid the trap of chasing endless goals without satisfaction, and they also avoid getting stuck in past successes while the world moves on.

Every win carries two responsibilities—honor it and use it. Honor it by giving it space, acknowledging the people and processes that made it possible. Use it by letting it fuel the next stage of your vision. That's how you turn achievements into stepping stones rather than final chapters. Over time, this approach builds not only a track record of success but a life and business that keep evolving without losing their spark.

Sustaining wealth isn't a finish line—it's an ongoing process of stewardship, adaptation, and smart decision-making. The systems you put in place today shape not only your financial freedom but also the opportunities you can create for others. With a clear plan, a willingness to keep learning, and the discipline to act on what you know, you position yourself to grow beyond survival or comfort and into significance. The aim is to build something that lasts—through market shifts, life changes, and the seasons ahead.

About the Author

Linda Caldwell is a dynamic entrepreneur and business strategist with a remarkable track record of empowering individuals to unlock their potential and achieve substantial financial success.

With over 15 years of experience in the business arena, she specializes in mentoring aspiring entrepreneurs to build six-figure businesses within just 12 months, all while establishing a foundation for generational wealth.

Hailing from the heart of Detroit, Linda embodies strength, passion, and influence. She is dedicated to nurturing emerging entrepreneurs through workshops, mentorship, and captivating conference presentations. Beyond her professional pursuits, Linda is a loving mother, devoted wife, doting grandmother, and compassionate foster parent.

Her resonant voice champions empowerment and purpose, inspiring those around her to transcend challenges and rise above their circumstances. Proudly embracing the title of 'jack of all trades,' she has mastered the art of resilience, forging an empire from adversity.

Passionate about financial empowerment, Linda is on a mission to help individuals and families secure their financial futures. With a deep belief in the power of generational wealth, she is committed to guiding other people toward financial independence.

Her book, ***'Unlocking Your Fortune'*** is a treasure-trove of wisdom, brimming with insights that illuminate the path to success in both business and life.

Your Future Can't Wait

You've just invested time in learning, growing, and dreaming bigger.

Now it's time to **put action behind that vision**.

> 📌 **If tomorrow came sooner than expected... would your family be ready?**
>
> 📌 **If an opportunity to grow your money was right in front of you... would you take it?**

I'm here to make sure your answer is **YES**—every single time.

💼 **For life insurance & annuity services that protect, grow, and preserve your legacy:**
👉 LindaKFinances.com – Schedule your private consultation today.

🎤 **For speaking engagements that inspire, empower, and transform audiences:**
👉 LindaKSpeaks.com – Let's make your next event unforgettable.

Your dreams are worth protecting. Your family is worth securing.

And you... are worth investing in.

Let's build your future—together.

Linda K. Caldwell

Your Partner in Wealth, Wisdom, and Legacy

www.ingramcontent.com/pod-product-compliance
Lightning Source LLC
LaVergne TN
LVHW022108200926
848481LV00003B/1111
* 9 7 9 8 3 4 9 2 1 1 7 6 8 *